HELPLESSLY
WATCHING
HANNAH

A FATHER'S STORY...

HELPLESSLY
WATCHING
HANNAH

A FATHER'S STORY...

ANDY DOWSON

First published in 2020 by Sixth Element Publishing
on behalf of Andy Dowson

Sixth Element Publishing
Arthur Robinson House
13-14 The Green
Billingham
Stockton on Tees
TS23 1EU
Tel: 01642 360253
www.6epublishing.net

ISBN 978-1-912218-90-5

British Library Cataloguing in Publication Data. A catalogue record for this
book is available from the British Library.

Printed in Great Britain.

To Alice, the little girl who would sit in the background, surrounded by monitors and wires. I listened to your stories of what you were going to do when your sister got better, as you hoped your little sister would come home and be able to play with you. You could not have been a better sister.

And to Nicola… I know how torn you felt as you tirelessly split your time between the girls, giving both our daughters the attention and care they needed. Thank you for being there when I couldn't be.

CONTENTS

CHAPTER 1

A Normal Saturday…
10th December 2005

It was just a normal Saturday morning, December 10th 2005. I had woken from a slight lie in after being at work all week for the local council, as well as carrying out my part-time job on an evening after work, cleaning carpets to make ends meet. Janine, my wife, was at work and her son Sean, who was ten years old, was in bed. I was looking forward to a night out in Redcar as one of my mates was having a few drinks before his wedding the following week.

Just then, the phone rang. To be honest, I had expected the call earlier as my two girls, Alice aged ten and Hannah aged seven, usually rang to say they wanted picking up from their mam's house to come round mine as we would usually do something for the day… me, Alice, Hannah, Sean and of course Patch the Jack Russell who lived with me at our house in Sandsend Road, Redcar, and who loved Hannah as much as she loved him. It was the normal thing. Nicola (Alice and Hannah's mam) had the kids sleeping at hers through the week, and they would stop at mine at the weekends or until they got bored and wanted to go back to their mam's house.

Whenever the kids arrived at mine, Alice would shoot off to watch TV or play with her Bratz dolls, whereas Hannah was animal-mad, and especially when it came to Patch. The love they had for each other was something I had never witnessed before.

Little did I realise that the phone call I was about to receive was to change my life forever. As I answered the phone, Nicola was clearly upset and couldn't get her words out. I could sense the panic in her voice and told her to slow down and tell me what was up. In the background I could hear Hannah crying, and Alice, at ten years old, reassuring her like she always had since she was three. I could hear the dogs, Mollie and Rosie, in the background, barking and being hysterical. The whole house seemed like it had just had a mad man run through and everyone inside that house was now suffering the consequences of it.

Nicola said, "Andrew, you need to get round here now. It's Hannah. She's blind. She can't see a thing."

I said, "Don't be so stupid. No one just goes blind. Calm yourself down and stop panicking."

"For god's sake," Nicola said, "please believe me. She can't see a thing. Her eyes are wide open."

Just then Nicola spoke to Hannah and I could hear her say in the calmest voice she had under the circumstances, "Hannah, open your eyes for mammy, that's a good girl now tell me if you can see anything now. Dad's on the phone."

Hannah replied, "Mam, I can't see anything, nothing at all. Believe me, please, help me."

My stomach was churning inside. I knew this was serious now. I had to get round there as soon as possible. I slammed the phone and ran into Sean's room and told him he had to get up quickly. I told him I'd drop him at his dad's around the corner, because Hannah was ill and I needed to get there. He quickly got dressed and I took him round the corner in the car. Unfortunately his dad wasn't in but his best friend Billy lived a few doors away so we headed there. I briefly explained what was happening to Billy's mam and dad and they took Sean off my hands.

I raced round to Hannah's to find a man and woman standing outside. I couldn't understand who they were or what they were doing there, but walked past them and knocked on the door. There was no answer, so I walked in.

Nicola shouted, "We're up here."

I could hear the noise and commotion so I ran up the stairs.

"Hannah, I'm here now," I said as calmly as I could. "Okay, I want you to look at me and tell me what you see."

She was crying hysterically.

Alice was clearly in shock along with Nicola.

"I can't see anything, dad," she said to me.

As a family, we were used to hospitals. Hannah had been in and out of hospital since she was five months old. But I can honestly say, at this point in my life, that morning was the scariest, most gut-wrenching feeling I had ever experienced. I had two tours of Northern Ireland under my belt from my Army days, and that experience, as bad as it had been, was nothing compared to how I felt right then with Hannah.

For quite some time now Hannah had been travelling to Newcastle RVI, which was around fifty miles away, twice a week for another treatment called plasma exchange in connection with her kidneys. But this new development was serious. I didn't know what to do, neither did Nicola.

She began ringing the hospital to speak to staff who knew Hannah and her past medical history, but it was Saturday and we were going to get nowhere. The people who knew Hannah were not around, and the only people Nicola could speak to were nurses who, as much as they would have liked to help, couldn't. They were just shocked at what Nicola was telling them.

We decided we would drive up to see the staff on ward seven personally in case the loss of sight was linked to the plasma exchange treatment. Hopefully they'd be there and able to help.

Alice would be once again shipped off to her Nana Norma, Nicola's mam, or Kendra, Nicola's sister, and would have to wait patiently for news of her sister after witnessing yet another emergency dash to the hospital, except this time it was different. I could see Alice was clearly frightened.

I sat with Hannah trying to reassure her as much as I

could. Nicola and Alice got ready. Norma came round as fast as she could. She needed to take Alice and take her quickly. I went outside and there stood the same people I had passed on the doorstep earlier.

It turned out they were there to change the mobility car. I couldn't believe it. I told them no, but they insisted. I very rarely lose my temper and am considered quite laid back. I looked at them and said absolutely nothing. The woman said it didn't matter and that we would do it another day. It must have been obvious that by the way I was looking at them that they knew they had to leave.

I got in my car and rang my wife Janine. There was no answer. Her phone must have been in her locker at work. Okay, I thought, I can call her later so she knows where she needs to pick Sean up from.

I went back in to Nicola's and helped get Hannah's coat on. Hannah was sobbing the whole time. I picked her up and carried her to the car. Nicola got in first, sat in the back and I placed Hannah on her mum's knee.

I got in the front seat and turned round before I turned the key. I said to Nicola, "Are you ready, seat belt on? Have you managed to get it round Hannah too?"

Nicola nodded, still shocked at what was going on, but still, like me, thinking no doubt in the back of her mind that this would be over soon, and Hannah's sight would come back by the time we reached Newcastle RVI surely.

I turned the key and drove off on what should have been a fifty mile, one hour journey. Little did I know that this was the start of a nine year journey that would end up with me coming close to a nervous breakdown as I stood there 95% of the time watching helplessly.

CHAPTER 2

A Typical Kid Growing Up To
Having Two Of My Own…
1960s – 1998

My early memories were spending time at nana and granddad's house in a village called Boosbeck in the North East of England, a mile from a village called Lingdale where I would spend most of my youth living with my three sisters and a brother, stepdad and mother. We didn't have a great deal but never went without. My stepdad Phil worked long hours in extreme conditions for the gas board. My mam usually did part time work to make sure we managed.

My real dad lived in the same village and was married to a woman who already had children. I saw him occasionally but I didn't ever see either him or my stepdad as my father figure, it was my granddad who I looked up to in this respect. He had made his money and retired fairly young but was continuously looking to make something here and there.

His big bungalow had land and this is where I always preferred to be, playing around and sitting listening to him about life and how I should make sure my family were always looked after when I was older and to make sure I didn't have to work till an old age, retire then keel over and die within a month or two of retirement.

Although he was my hero, he could be full of hot air at times, promising me this and that but not always delivering when it came to mini motorbikes, and other outrageous items any kid would love. Nana was great, she always looked out for me but knew I was granddad's favourite. Her favourite was Elizabeth, my older sister. We would all go round to nana and granddad's every Sunday for a bath in my early years when we lived at Boosbeck because our house in Fenton Street didn't have a bath, and just had an outside toilet.

All in all, my granddad was the man who laid the foundations for me as a child and he was the man I looked to be like one day – house, land, retired early but most importantly a strong father figure who loved his kids.

During my youth growing up and living in Lingdale, I met friends I grew up with, friends who would always be there for me if needed. The people of Lingdale are a great set of people with a great community spirit. We had lots to do as kids. If we weren't on the shale heap riding old Hondas (Honda Grandads, one up three down gears), we were up the quarry on the Tarzan swings, or down Moorsholm Wood in the beck. Failing that, we were playing football, birds nesting, or on our push bikes somewhere between Brotton, Skelton, Stanghow, Castelton, Margrove Park, Charlton's and Boosbeck, the surrounding villages of Lingdale. There were no video games except the Atari, and the problem with that was you would insert a cartridge before going to school, come home and it was maybe at 95% loaded. By the time it got to 100% it was too late, your mam had made you tea (dinner for those from the south of England), washed the pots and wanted to sit and watch Coronation Street so she needed the TV.

The street houses in Lingdale were being demolished and the occupants were being moved from a two up two down to Cedarhurst Drive and Meadowdale Court, two nice estates with gardens front and rear. This was probably my best time growing up in Lingdale. There was a gang of us: Nick, Titchy, Wacky and Pogo and a couple of others. We would go in to the old houses and just smash them to bits, the old outside toilets, kitchens. It was brilliant. We would go up in the lofts and walk through the lofts up the whole street, knocking down the thin walls in between each house. That wasn't the worst thing we did.

I admit, growing up, I wasn't the most pleasant of lads at times, and there are parts of my life I would rather forget, things I said and did. I would subconsciously say to myself, "I hope to god I never have a son like me. I hope when I eventually marry and settle down I have girls." God forbid I'd have another Andy Dowson being a nuisance as he grew up.

The village bobby did knock at the door now and again, but this was very rare. Mam would open the door to him, he would begin a sentence about me regarding

9

some stupid prank I'd pulled or someone I'd upset, then he'd get a whiff of what mam was baking and simply say, "Ah Joan, is that carrot cake I can smell?" She would in turn quickly go to the kitchen, whip open the oven, cut him a piece and hand it to him at the door. He would stand and eat it. Problem solved as he wiped his chin with the back of his hand, dust down his uniform of any crumbs, hand the empty plate back and then say to mam, "Just have a word with Andrew, will you? Tell him and the gang he hangs out with to behave." And that was that.

I worked from an early age. First it was a paper round six nights a week, then six mornings too, then I went on to the Sunday morning papers also so in total I was delivering the papers six nights and seven mornings and receiving £5.40. I was rich in 1984, or at least I thought I was.

In my final two years at school I got a job on the milk round two mornings a week, Saturday mornings and Monday mornings before school, so I had to ditch the paper rounds. I wasn't bothered though because now I was receiving £9.00 a week. I was loaded. On a Monday I would pack my uniform in a bag in case the milk round ran over. Marian, the milk lady, would be driving down Stanghow Road, flashing her lights from the Datsun milk van at the school coach as it pulled off, telling them to stop as she had me standing on the back of the milk. I would then jump off, and jump on the bus and get changed into my school uniform while on the bus.

School finished and I was awarded an apprenticeship whilst all my mates went on to a £27.30 a week Youth Training Scheme (YTS). I was on £54.00 a week, and I believe one of the reasons I was offered this was because of the work I was doing before I left school as the interviewer realised the work ethic I could produce due to the jobs I did before leaving school. He wasn't interested that I would be leaving school with no qualifications. However after a few months I knew it wasn't for me, talking to men who had stood at the same machine for thirty years smoking rollies, talking about the settings of the machine all day. I needed more adventure.

I knew I needed to get out of the village, and there was only one place: the local Army Infantry Regiment, The Green Howards.

Training was tough. I was the youngest in the platoon at seventeen years old and but was only one of fifteen, of the original forty four that had started six months previously, to complete the training.

After completing my training, that was it... Northern Ireland awaited. It was 1989, things were settling down but that didn't stop us looking for trouble when out patrolling the streets of Londonderry. I met some great friends in the Army including some of the biggest wind up merchants in the world, and we ran pranks that matched anything me and the gang in East Cleveland had ever pulled.

As well as two tours of Northern Ireland during the

troubles, once in South Armagh (bandit country) and once in Londonderry, I did a four month tour of the Falkland Islands where we managed to spread the rumour of a mock garrison call out that had the whole island including the RAF squadron and radar station staff all kitted up and waiting for the call at 5am. We didn't admit to that one until we left the island.

I decided to leave the Army in 1992 aged 21. I'd had enough. I knew I could have risen through the ranks but I'd seen enough, it wasn't for me any more. I was seeing mates meet women from Catterick or Richmond fall in love, get married and then be living in the married quarters at twenty years old, yet they'd only met three months before. No wonder the divorce rate was so high. I didn't want that. I was single, young and happy. I came home from Northern Ireland in one piece, my mind was still sharp and I decided I would leave the Army and become a millionaire. Well, that's what I said to myself. Up until now that still hasn't happened.

After leaving the Army, I met Nicola a few months later. We dated for a while then moved in together, everything I was against while I was in the Army, the only difference was we weren't married. After three years together we planned to have a child and along came Alice, eight pound thirteen ounces on October 24th 1995 at 7.13am. The feeling which I'm sure every father feels is unreal and unexplainable. It was at this point I said to myself, no matter what happens in the future, I am always going to be there for my children no matter what. Even though having kids wasn't really at the top of my agenda to be perfectly honest, I just seemed to go along with the flow. However when Alice arrived, everything changed.

What immediately struck me was how much of a good mother Nicola was. She took to it like a duck to water. Alice and Nicola were so close it was unreal. I would take Alice to my allotment when she was toddling where she would walk around with the chickens, ducks and dogs I had. She loved it and so did I. Whenever I came back from work, Alice would want to come to the allotment. Off we would go, Alice on my shoulders and a couple of dogs following us down to the garden where we would spend hours together. No mobile phones for people looking for me or Nicola ringing to tell us to come back for dinner… we would return when we wanted.

The thought of a second child coming along seemed like a good idea at the time and we decided another child may sort the niggling problems we were having in our relationship at the time, so along came Hannah.

She was born July 20th 1998, a healthy baby weighing eight pound eleven ounces. It was a bright sunny day and she arrived during the adverts of Coronation Street. It's funny these things you remember but in the background the adverts started on the hospital TV and when she arrived I could hear the music come back on in the background.

Immediately the relevant people were informed of the arrival and the usual checks were carried out. Nothing stood out as a problem so we were happy that Alice had a sister and how much fun they would have over the years to come. The birth of Hannah was much quicker and more straightforward than Alice's birth. Alice had taken forever to arrive some three years earlier, or it seemed that way.

Hannah arrived home some days later after spending a few extra days in hospital with jaundice, understood to be quite common so there were no alarms raised and we didn't think anything of it.

We lived in our two up two down house in Queen Street, Boosbeck, but knew in time we would outgrow it. I had just started a new job on the local authority and wasn't in a position to move house to something bigger due to the job being a short term contract, however I took a gamble, bought a bigger house in Redcar town and rented out the one we were in at Boosbeck. It was a huge gamble and if I had been laid off at the end of the contract, we were in trouble. However it didn't turn out that way and the contract was extended.

In between work I would be at home decorating and making the house liveable, and eventually we got close to the point of moving in in order to have our first Christmas at home in a new house.

The holidays were just round the corner. Hannah was about five months old and she was a little under the weather but the previous day she had been videoed lying on her back, kicking her feet and laughing with her cousin Charlie who was born five days after her.

Nicola decided to walk into town with her sister Kendra

who was having Charlie meet the nurse to have her Hib and Polio jabs. Nicola had Hannah booked in for the next session and decided to omit the jabs due to Hannah being a little under the weather. Just for courtesy, she popped her head around the corner of the office as her sister went through the door with Charlie.

Nicola explained to the nurse she wouldn't be getting Hannah's jabs today as she was unwell. At this point she was reassured by the nurse and told to not worry, Hannah would be fine and with it being so close to Christmas it was best to get them done and out of the way.

After she had the jab, Hannah slept right the way through to the next morning but we weren't concerned as Hannah was a good sleeper. The next day was a Friday and it was the works Christmas party. Kendra was babysitting. Hannah had been off colour and quiet the whole day, but we went to the party and received a call one hour in to come home as Kendra was concerned about Hannah.

We immediately got home. Kendra was right. Hannah was not herself. We called the doctor who advised that she would be okay and that children regularly react like this to an immunisation. The next morning Nicola's mam Norma came round. Hannah was sitting in her lean back bouncy chair, trying to reach the baubles on the Christmas tree. Two days before she was knocking them all over, today she couldn't lift her arms. Norma said we needed to get Hannah to the doctors.

We went backwards and forwards listening to doctors reassuring two young parents that Hannah would be okay, but late that night we knew something wasn't right and again went to the doctor. He could see we were worried and admitted Hannah to hospital.

We arrived at the hospital 9.30pm on December 18th 1998. Little did we know that from this date, James Cook University Hospital (JCUH) would become Hannah's second home for the next fifteen and a half years.

CHAPTER 3

A Turn For The Worse...
December 18th 1998 – February 20th 1999

Hannah was really ill. We could see this and we were concerned. For the next two days we sat in a cubicle with her. She couldn't move. I remember a team of doctors coming round, observing Hannah, and at one point the doctor picked her up and her body just flopped like a rag doll.

They were confused. We could see it in their faces, which didn't reassure us at all. We were new to this environment and couldn't understand why this was happening. Time after time the doctors would come in and ask what had happened over the last few days and all we could explain was that we thought an immunisation may have triggered this episode. This was the only thing we could think, however we were told that it had nothing to do with it. I was frustrated and at one point said to a doctor, "Rubbish, you mean to tell me that a perfectly healthy baby with a sniffle becomes paralysed overnight yet the immunisation had nothing at all to do with it?" I was always met with a reassuring answer that the jab played no part.

In the early hours of December 20th, things took a turn for the worse. Hannah could only whimper. Not only had she lost all feeling in her body but now her vocal chords had gone. A very concerned nurse, who had the job of looking after six children, had focused her attention on Hannah and wouldn't leave her for the last few hours. She called the on duty consultant and immediately Hannah was admitted to the Paediatric Intensive Care Unit (PICU). Hannah was dying.

She was put on a life support machine, tubes coming out of her nose, wires everywhere, monitors with numbers and lines crossing horizontally across the screen, constantly showing peaks and troughs in their identification.

This is the worst nightmare that you can have, and here we were living it, feeling so hopeless. What could we do? When was someone going to tell us what was going on? Eventually a lady came to see us and explained the situation in the best way she could. She would become Hannah's consultant (Senior Doctor) and it was clear she knew what she was talking about. Her name was Fiona Hampton, and not only did she become Hannah's consultant, but she was also a very good sounding board, and a good person to be in charge of Hannah's development. We all had a lot of respect for each other. She saved Hannah from the jaws of death so many times. Fiona was probably the best consultant I have ever had the privilege to meet.

I had to go back to work before breaking up for the Christmas period, but after a couple of days I received a call from Nicola asking me to come straight up to the hospital as Fiona wanted to see me. I'd been visiting after work but was in touch constantly. Deep down subconsciously I knew this time was serious. Alice was having the time of her life. She was only three and didn't understand what was going on. Nursery had broken up and Alice was at the hospital in the playroom, playing with all the children and making new friends, whilst her mam sat by Hannah's bed.

The conversation to come was one of the worst a parent can have and it was the first of many to come as Hannah continued to baffle the world of medicine. I could see Nicola was falling apart. We sat around Hannah's bed, myself, Nicola, Fiona and, at the foot of the bed, a named nurse who was solely tasked with looking after Hannah, sitting at a mini desk with Hannah's notes. And then there was Hannah, laid in bed, wired up to the ventilator, her life-support machine.

The conversation began with reference to Hannah's condition and how numerous tests were being done but whilst they waited for results they said Hannah's condition was not good and there was a strong possibility that she may not survive this and we should prepare for the worst. There had been a steady decline in her condition which wasn't showing signs of improvement. I couldn't take this in and began to cry. The last time I cried was when Hannah was born. That was five months earlier and was tears of joy, now I was crying as I was possibly going to lose my daughter.

On Christmas Eve, Nicola stayed with Hannah for as long as she could then left to prepare Alice for Christmas as we were trying to make it as enjoyable as possible for her, even though the circumstances were just heartbreaking. I stayed at the hospital by Hannah's bed and was going to be there for Hannah's first Christmas.

Hannah's named nurse for that night was a man called Mike Carr, a man who would play a pivotal part in Hannah's wellbeing over the next few years and a man who I can say I have so much respect for. We started to chat about life in general. The ward was quiet. Just then I heard carol singers in the background somewhere in the hospital and didn't give it a second thought. But then I turned round to see around ten carol singers outside the PICU doorway. They began to sing Silent Night to the children in the ward, however there was only Hannah in that night. I put my head down and cried and cried like I had never cried before. Mike tried to reassure me as they sang the whole Christmas carol, but it was no use, I had to let it all out. I was beside myself thinking how could this be happening to my daughter, and most of all why?

I felt weak crying so much but I couldn't stop. Inside I was saying to myself, "Pull yourself together, man," but it was no use. Everything hit me so hard, I just couldn't stop, head bowed, tears flowing, it was no use, I had to let it out.

I left the hospital just after midnight. I leaned over Hannah's bed, kissed her, told her I loved her and wished her a happy Christmas and hoped she would have many more. I went home feeling so low, but knew I had to switch from sad to happy as Alice would be awake in a few hours, excited about Christmas.

Christmas morning went very quickly with Alice. While she opened her presents, in another corner of the room were Hannah's unopened presents.

We all arrived at the hospital later that day to a still critical baby. Some humour was injected into the day by a nurse called Karen, someone who was always the life and soul of the ward. With a contagious sense of humour, she was the key to that day, making it as enjoyable as could be. At one point she put on a Russian hat and tap danced which left me in hysterics. Karen would be a part of Hannah's life for the next fifteen and a half years, and also play a major part in the end.

As Christmas Day went by, Nicola's relatives came and went. I played with Alice in the playroom with her new presents. She should have been at home but she knew in her little brain we had to be up here for her sister. Sometime later we all left together.

The next week went by with no change and no answers, then on January 1st 1999 Hannah's condition improved slightly. By this time I knew the screens and the observation charts so I would arrive and look at the notes and ask questions to be told how things were going. I was happier and thought, great, we're going to get back the Hannah we had two weeks ago. Unfortunately we were going to get her back but her mobility had been damaged and there was a long road ahead. Hannah was then to have a tracheostomy fitted which meant her breathing would be helped by inserting a tube into her throat, so the tubes would be removed from her nose.

This wasn't the end of the world because as she got stronger it would be removed and as she grew older there would be no sign at all of where the tube was inserted in to her throat.

Hannah was improving slightly. Physio needed to be taught and organised, special splints to hold Hannah's feet in position were made, and she also now needed grommets inserted into her ears to help her hearing.

It was now nearly eight weeks Hannah had been in hospital. I had gone back to work after the Christmas break. Norma was helping with Alice, and Nicola was spending many hours a day at the hospital. I would come up the hospital after work and do my share of sitting by Hannah's bed and generally getting to know all the staff.

When it was time for Hannah to go home, we left with a one page piece of paper on what to do, a list of medical equipment and medicines, and a promise of frequent visits from the community nurse to enable the care needed to be performed so Hannah could move on and have a fulfilling life. We were naïve parents and didn't have a clue how to cope. We had Alice who needed us and, being the dad, I had to show them that we would be okay. I was relieved but scared to death on what the future was going to bring.

CHAPTER 4

Blue-lighted to Newcastle Royal Victoria Hospital (RVI)…
October 1999

Almost a year later, there was another development. Hannah had not been well for a few days, looking weak. Her pallor was wrong and quite rightfully so I was worried and so was Nicola. It was October 1999, nearly eight months after her previous visit to JCUH so we took Hannah back there and after the usual long wait in the day unit, we eventually got to speak to a doctor.

Over the next hour we recited Hannah's history as the doctor carefully examined her at great length. We could see that the doctors were baffled so a senior consultant was called who advised on bloods being taken and analysed. The doctor didn't think she warranted a stay so we were then sent home.

When we got home I decided to call a friend and was on the phone for nearly an hour explaining what had happened with Hannah and that we could see she was unwell yet we had been sent home and was quite annoyed with them, especially given Hannah's history.

No sooner had I put the phone down and the phone rang. It was a doctor telling me to get Hannah and get back up to the hospital immediately and all would be explained when we got there, however the emphasis was on 'immediately'.

I didn't need to explain to Nicola. She knew by the look on my face. Norma was called to come and collect Alice, who was sorting an overnight bag and looking forward to spending a night at nana and granddad's, yet still concerned and dealing with the issue in her own little way.

We packed the car and set off, reaching the hospital around thirty minutes later to be confronted by a consultant who explained that Hannah had shown signs of renal failure and Newcastle RVI was to be her next location to treat this as JCUH didn't have the resources to deal with child renal failure. Renal failure? What was that? It was her kidneys. They were failing, and failing fast. We were to head up to the hospital quickly with a blue light flashing. This was serious.

The ambulance was waiting, Nicola boarded with Hannah, and I was to follow behind with the car as we needed transport at the hospital. The journey took around an hour. The whole time the blue light was flashing and I was behind the ambulance. At times other cars had to pull over to let the ambulance pass and then when I passed in my Ford Mondeo, some would beep and flash, thinking no doubt I was jumping the traffic and using the ambulance to my advantage. However anyone with half a brain would have realised I was a relative.

The journey was long and it gave me too much time to think. What if she died? Why was I on the phone at home for so long? The doctor could have rung earlier and we wouldn't need to have been in such a rush? How could I have been so stupid? What about Alice? How was she? Would she be okay?

It was around 9pm, a cold night and miserable night so the weather didn't help my mood. I was alone with lots of time to think and eventually I began to cry as I was driving. I was telling myself, it was okay, I couldn't embarrass myself as no one could see or know I'd been upset. As soon as I arrived at the hospital I'd switch back on to be the supporting dad and grown up adult. I can't get upset, I was thinking, it's not the normal thing to do.

When we arrived at the hospital, Hannah was sleeping so she was carried into the hospital where we were directed toward ward seven, the Children's Renal Unit. The hospital was old but well kept. There was a feeling of urgency as we were making our ways through long, never-ending corridors that were quiet due to the time of night. Whenever I hear a certain song called 'Wires' by the group Athlete, it saddens me to the core as it reminds me of that night in 1999 travelling through the hospital, as apparently the lead singer wrote it about his child when he also attended hospital.

The staff were great and introduced themselves, trying to make it as welcoming as they could. We were shown to a private booth where tests were done immediately on Hannah, and consultants were advising us on the plan and possible consequences of Hannah's illness if they didn't act now.

The first part of the plan was to carry out a blood

transfusion. This worked well. Hannah looked and seemed great. I was happy and so was Nicola, however there were underlying issues we couldn't see on the surface, yet the experts could, and they then told us of another plan and this involved a sort of dialysis treatment known in the industry as plasma exchange. I'm not a medical genius and would never claim to be, but the way I understood it is this: Hannah was linked up to a machine, her bloods were taken and cleaned as they went through a system then went back in to her body. Although my summary sounds simple enough, the process involves lots of tests that can make the child feel unwell.

During the stay, one parent was allowed to sleep by Hannah's bed and if another parent stayed there was a large house called Crawford House, sponsored by the actor Michael Crawford, which had all the facilities.

It was here that parents could take time to relax away from the hospital and it even had a playroom for siblings of the sick children. On occasions, parents would bring their sick children to play there if they were either getting ready for discharge or feeling better. During the stay there, it was sad at times as you would see a child walking in with their parents, pulling along a transfusion bottle on a trolley, and sometimes children would be seen with no hair, obviously going through chemotherapy.

During the stay at Crawford house while sitting in the lounge, I met a man from my home town who was there with his child who had contracted meningitis and unfortunately had many amputations on parts of his limbs. I also met a man from the Lake District whose daughter was suffering from cancer. We spoke briefly about both our children's illness then he left rather abruptly. It was obvious he needed to go back to his room as he was becoming emotional and, like me, he felt no doubt that he had to keep it together and not be seen to cry as it was maybe seen as a sign of weakness.

Fathers could be seen holding it together and talking about the manly things we men do, but I knew each one I spoke to was hurting so bad inside but keeping it together for the sake of the mother and child. As a father who had been in so much pain myself, I could see it automatically.

During my stay, I was called in to an office to speak to a lady whose son had died many years before from kidney failure. She introduced herself and explained that she had become a leader in improving the kidney research and then asked me how I was coping? I held it together and told her it was a struggle getting back and forward to and from the hospital, financially and emotionally. A one hundred mile round trip every other day juggling work, Alice and the hospital was becoming a problem and we just hoped to be home soon.

She handed me a cheque for £50 towards petrol money. I couldn't believe it. I explained that I couldn't afford to repay her immediately but would pay £10 back a week. She laughed and said, "This is from the Kidney foundation, not from me personally." To this day, if I ever enter any charity shop down town, it's the Kidney Research shop, and if I do browse, I'll buy something, because I know there may be a parent out there who may be passed on the money to help them in times of need, and trust me, this was a time of need for us.

Over the weeks, Hannah started to look like she was on the mend. We were all happy. A consultant said prior to our departure in the debrief meeting that this was probably a fluke illness and if by any chance Hannah was to have a relapse it would be in the next five years. We left the hospital after three weeks, looking forward to celebrating the new millennium with a fit and healthy Hannah. It was like she had never been unwell.

CHAPTER 5

Back To Square One And Moving Forwards…
2000 – 2003

The millennium year had gone remarkably well. Hannah had no admissions to hospitals for her previous illnesses and things were looking up, although Hannah's mobility was restricted due to the first ever illness. She had trouble with the joints of her ankles which meant that, where we can sit and raise our feet up and down, Hannah had no control of this action so she needed splints to support her ankle and keep it rigid to walk.

This was a struggle. She was two years old and already behind so we set about getting her to walk with the aid of the splints and she managed, a little unstable at times but we got there in the end. Her cheeky character was starting to shine through and although she was registered disabled, this didn't bother any of us in the least as a barrier for her going through life as normal. She was provided a frame with wheels to support her so she would be seen whizzing up and down the aisles while shopping or smashing in to everything in the house. Everybody who came into contact with her instantly warmed to her. You couldn't help but love her.

Alice would always be there in the background when

people spoke to Hannah but it was evident that Hannah took centre stage. This didn't seem to bother Alice as she was always making sure Hannah was okay. However when Hannah became frustrated, it was Alice who was on the receiving end of the frustration, but as time went on it was evident that Alice was there to help Hannah whenever she needed it. If Hannah fell over, Alice would be there to pick her up, or run to inform either me or Nicola that Hannah needed help.

Hannah became mad on videos, mainly Toy Story and would watch it time and time again while Alice played with her dolls or danced. It was also around this time we noticed how much Hannah loved animals. It was strange how they seemed to interact with her as if they knew she wasn't the same as everyone else. We bought a small Yorkshire terrier for both Alice and Hannah. They both adored it, and sometime later we decide to get another Yorkshire terrier, which was born November 15th 2000 and could leave its mother around Christmas. As it was evident that Hannah was the animal lover, we decided that the puppy could be given to Hannah on Christmas morning.

Hannah and Alice had both opened their presents together. Only two years earlier we had been told to expect the worse. Alice had been too young to be really unaware of the seriousness of the situation then. But on this occasion it was a time to celebrate the fact Hannah was alive and there to open her Christmas presents together with her sister. As the puppy was so small, we decided to place the puppy in a small tin and hand the tin to Hannah to open the lid. The puppy had been in the back kitchen with Rosie the other dog all night so Hannah and Alice knew nothing of the new pup as it had been collected late Christmas Eve. Nicola placed the pup inside the tin, closed the lid and walked into the front room to hand it to Hannah who looked at her blankly. Nicola told her to open it. She just thought it was a small teddy of some kind until it moved.

The look on both kids' faces that day was priceless. Hannah fell in love with the dog that day and would be seen later on walking with the pup and Rosie inside a double buggy up and down the street. One such photo was published in the Evening Gazette when a story was released on Hannah's escape from death due to her illnesses. They would be brought up to the hospital many times throughout the years to visit Hannah. They were her life. She loved them while at the same time when she was healthy she'd tease them. She would block an escape route at the back of the settee, chase the dogs behind and tease the life out of them. They would growl and snarl at her as they were trapped and couldn't escape but they would never bite her.

There was a worry that Hannah's hearing wasn't as good as it should be, so as a precaution grommets had been inserted in to her ears some time ago. I was reassured this was routine and thought no more of it. Although throughout the time she had these inserted she seemed to get quite a few ear infections. I constantly asked the question, "Is there a possibility the grommets are causing this? It's the same ear." I was told no and like many fathers out there, looking back I feel I was being ignored or not being listened to.

It was around Easter 2001 that Hannah became ill with another ear infection. This was different. The symptoms were beginning to look a lot like the episode in 1998 when she became floppy. It was no normal ear infection so we rushed her to hospital and within hours she was deteriorating again. She was assessed and was sedated. There was a meeting called and we were told that we may lose Hannah. I knew deep down it was the grommets that were the reason for the infection, due to her immune system being susceptible to infections. It was the reason her system shut down after another infection.

Hannah was sedated for just over three weeks, Easter came and went, during which time the bikers turned up with Easter eggs and came round the wards talking to the sick kids. I've always had a great deal of respect for the bikers from that day.

Here poor Hannah was again back to square one, life in the balance. Nicola was constantly at her bedside, I was juggling work to keep me occupied, taking Alice to school in between work, and with nana and granddad looking after Alice again, I went up to see Hannah lying there, asking the questions about the monitors and locking my thoughts away.

Alice would also be at the hospital a lot when she wanted to be around her mam, Hannah and me. She has spent so many years meeting kids on the ward and playing with them in the playroom and craft room, keeping herself occupied while we tried to balance things out for both time spent with Alice and Hannah. It's funny looking back because some of the nurses have been there forever and remember Alice coming in the ward at three years old. Now she is a grown woman it's unbelievable just how long she has been going up to the hospital to sit and wait for either me or her mam.

Hannah was fitted with a tracheostomy for breathing after another two months in hospital. This was fitted to allow her to breathe without the help of a ventilator, which also meant she could come home when time allowed with an abundance of equipment which was needed throughout the night to help with feeding and breathing.

It was my turn to stay at the hospital one night and early in the morning I received a knock at the door at the parents' room. I was told that Hannah was coming round from her sedation, which was to be expected as the settings had been reduced on the ventilator. I quickly got ready and went in to the ward. She couldn't move and was on her side. She was looking directly at me. She noticed me immediately and her big brown eyes widened. I looked at her, stroked her face and kissed her cheek. "Dad's here now," I said. "I'm staying. I love you and I've missed you." She couldn't talk because of the tracheostomy but she cried a whimper cry, no sound just the movement of her mouth. I told her it was okay and that she had been asleep for a long time, and mam would be up soon.

I said to her, "I'm going to put Toy Story on for you." Her mouth closed immediately, she stopped crying and she knew in her little mind it was going to be okay. That day she watched the film over and over again.

As the weeks went by, her movement came back slowly and allowed us to move with her to another ward, which was known as the High Dependency Unit (HDU). There are three categories which identify the level of care your child needs or seriousness of the illness: on the ward itself, HDU & PICU.

Being on the ward meant a doctor had assessed you and you would share a room with four other kids, and parents would stay the night and sleep on a bed by the side of you. It could be that you had been on the ward because you were getting better and had been on HDU, or PICU previously. As a general rule you had one nurse looking after maybe four to eight children.

In HDU you had your own room and had a nurse who would cater for you and maybe one or two other children, whereas on PICU you had one dedicated nurse twenty four hours a day. Over the years I have seen children come in to the PICU, then on to HDU, then on to the ward, running around only to go home okay. This was never the case with Hannah. The furthest she went was HDU. It was something that ate away at me, how I always thought throughout her life, "That poor girl, why her?"

It was around this time she had her first visit to Great

Ormond Street (GOS) and was eventually diagnosed with an illness called Chronic Intermittent Demyelinating Polyneurothopy (CIDP). Nicola had travelled down in the back of an ambulance with a nurse to be delivered to GOS for tests. This wouldn't be the only time Hannah went there, she would go again in 2006.

For over a year there was no sound from Hannah as the tracheostomy stopped any sound. She cried and you couldn't hear her, she laughed, nothing. During this time Hannah was slowly coming to terms with the tracheostomy. Over time you could hear slight noises from her which was due to the reduction in the tracheostomy's size as it allowed some noise through.

Not only did Hannah have a tracheostomy, she also had a feeding tube in her stomach. A tube was connected to this and then a test tube was connected to the tube. A special milk would be poured into the tube and you would lower the tube after unclasping the flow clip to allow gravity to take its place. The higher the tube, the faster the milk would flow causing Hannah to wretch, so it was important to get the right speed for her comfort.

Prior to this she had a tube inserted up her nose and then down to her stomach. You would push a tube up her nose then it would follow the flow of the back of the nose, going down the throat and in to the stomach. When it reached a certain point, the inside of the tube was pulled from the outer sheath leaving a hollow tube, which was then taped to the side of her cheek. The same principle was used in attaching a test tube and pouring milk into the test tube.

She would try and chat away with her tracheostomy in place. Over time I understood her conversation and learned to lip read well. It was difficult for us both as I'm sure it was for everyone else who communicated with Hannah. The decision was made by the hospital consultants that Hannah was to have her tracheostomy removed in 2002. Hannah went into the theatre to have it removed while we sat outside. After an hour or so we heard a cry. Although both me and Nicola had not heard Hannah's voice for so long, we knew that cry, it was over a year since it was heard last. As Nicola and I approached Hannah, she was crying loudly, but stopped when she saw her mam and me and began talking out loud. She was as shocked as we were as parents to hear her voice. The grommets had been removed also during the tracheostomy removal. The anaesthetist confirmed that a foreign body, i.e. the grommets, could well have caused the initial infection. Once again I had not been listened to.

Alice and Hannah would talk to each other for days after Hannah's voice had returned. It was good to see, and once again Hannah was on the way back.

It was during this time a holiday to Ibiza was organised, no tracheostomy, the wound had healed perfectly so it wouldn't cause an issue when Hannah would be in the water swimming. The holiday was eventful but fun. It was the last time we would holiday together as a family, as the strain of Hannah's illness and other contributing factors would cause me and Nicola to separate weeks after the holiday.

The break-up became messy and should never have been for kids to witness. There was a lot of taking sides and passing judgement. Access to the kids became difficult and I had to attend court on two separate occasions but I was going to be there for my kids, no matter what obstacles were thrown in my path.

It was strange at first when I would take the kids out alone. Two girls? What could I do with them? This is when our adventures started. We would go anywhere and everywhere. I would have the kids and they knew there would be no arguing between me and Nicola to contend with, and I'm sure they thought exactly the same when they went with their mam.

Hannah and Alice would get along fine most of the time, but like most children that age, around five and seven, they would fight and it was funny to watch occasionally. Despite everything they'd been through, they were typical kids. Alice was very protective of her little sister. But Hannah? Hannah was fearless.

On one occasion I went to pick up Hannah, Alice was away on holiday with her nana and granddad. As I came round the corner, I saw Hannah standing with a bike. I told her she had to be careful as it had no stabilisers on. Because of her having splints on her legs, she was slower at putting her legs down to regain her balance so it was suggested she should always have stabilisers.

Hannah then said, "Watch this, dad." My heart was in my mouth, but I watched, and off she went. Her mam had taught her to ride that day. It was another milestone, something that we were told would never happen. After that there was no stopping her. She couldn't keep up with her friends on foot, but on her bike she was with them and keeping up with them the whole time.

She would come and stay at my house in Redcar at the time and she and Alice would go up and down the street on the bikes. Hannah was in her element and so was Alice, as they could now ride their bikes together. Things were going in the right direction for once. I was single and enjoying myself but not forgetting my parental duties at the same time. It was difficult due to me and Nicola living so close. Although this was easier for the kids, I decided I needed to distance myself and went to live at my dad's house which he rented to me at Lingdale, as he was running a pub in a village called Roxby. The kids would come and stay at alternate weekends, and in the winter months we would go sledging up in the surrounding hills of Lingdale. It was around this time my neighbour Martin Wood, who owned the local butcher shop, suggested I take the kids on his daughters' horses, another adventure the kids loved.

When I had the kids Saturday afternoon till Sunday afternoon, we would go to the Lingdale Tavern. A lot of the parents would take their kids in there after the football. I would have a drink or two while the kids would all play. Around 7pm when the locals started to come in, it was time for the kids to leave so we would head home, and they would play until it was bedtime. On either a Saturday or Sunday morning while the kids were at mine, we would go on some kind of adventure, Lingdale Quarry, the woods, Castleton to the river, horse riding, or even to visit my nana. Her doorbell was so low they could reach it and so they would call her Nana Doorbell. There was never a time we did nothing. It was great.

CHAPTER 6

Swimming With Dolphins, Disneyland Florida…
June – July 2004

By summer 2004, I had been living alone for over a year or so, back in my old area, and had started dating someone new, Janine, who got on brilliantly with the girls. The kids were coming to my house every weekend. All was going well. Janine would come up at weekends after the kids were back at their mam's. It was great. Hannah was six that summer, and she was fit and well most of the time. She was quick witted and fun to be around. Alice was always with her, sharing the same wit and always there to help her when she needed a hand, whether it be to put on her splints or just be the brilliant sister she was. Every weekend we would be doing something different, picnics, beach, dog walking. Hannah and Alice had the two pet dogs, Molly and Rosie, the two Yorkshire terriers. Hannah would either place them in her twin buggy and walk them everywhere or just have them follow her wherever she went.

In the summer of that year, I had the opportunity to apply for a new job, the parks and countryside supervisor, on the council working for a respected man in the council called Ged Demoily. The day I got the call I was standing in my kitchen with Alice and Hannah. The phone rang two hours after the interview. I told the kids to be quiet, and then answered, expecting to be told the job had been offered to somebody else. I prepared myself, then boom, "We would like to offer you the role if you accept." After the phone call, I was jumping up and down as the kids did the same. Things were looking up. I had a new job.

I quickly fixed the problems in the parks and countryside with the team, I streamlined some of the routes and swapped people onto a rota system so they were doing a different route each week. The team had some great strengths. I saved the council a lot of money and I developed the team further to allow them to be more flexible. As time progressed this job also allowed me time to concentrate on my college course which was leadership and management and developed my skill set further.

It was around this time I decided to borrow some money from the property I owned in Boosbeck and organise a trip to Disneyland Florida, just for me, Alice and Hannah. It was booked for June 2004. The lead up to it was around nine months, and every time Hannah had a slight illness, the usual would happen, my heart would be in my mouth wondering if she was to be okay and more so if she would be able to go to Florida.

The holiday came round and we flew from Manchester Airport, the kids were excited and couldn't wait. We arrived in Florida mid-afternoon. As we approached the passport control, I was pulled aside and literally interrogated while the kids stood there, looking worried that something was wrong, I had to prove the place we were staying at, the tickets for the parks, the tickets to see the dolphins at discovery cove. I kept my cool and kept smiling to the kids to reassure them that it was okay. It didn't help that Hannah disappeared, only to be seen stroking the drug detection dog. Finally after spending over an hour convincing the authorities I was taking the children on holiday and had not abducted them, we were allowed to leave the airport, find the hire car and commence on our journey to start a two week adventure.

Within minutes of arriving at the apartment, Alice and Hannah had emptied their suitcases onto the floor, found their bathing suits and were off to the pool, leaving me to sort the clothes out and put them into the drawers.

That first day we stayed in the pool till the guy came and kicked us out. It was 11pm but still warm. We were having the time of our lives.

The next day we woke up and headed for breakfast at a nearby café and then began our attack on the parks. The first one involved us going on a safari where a vehicle drove us around a mock game park with real life animals. While we were waiting in the queue, Hannah had to sit in her wheelchair as her legs were becoming weak so the wheelchair came with us everywhere. When we reached the front of the queue, a lady from the staff came up to me and asked, "Why have you waited in the queue? You must never queue throughout Disneyland Florida if your child or any of your party has a disability." It was news to me, but was an added advantage as we had stood for over one hour and I knew after a few days the kids would start to get restless.

The drive to the parks always went up a road called the 192. From the car window, Hannah would watch a ball being catapulted into the air with two people inside and would say every day, "Dad, I want to go on that." There was no way that was going to happen. She was too young and it didn't look safe for a five year old. Adults yes, but a child? No way. Well, that was my thought at the time.

We spent most of the time at the water parks, Blizzard Beach and Typhoon Lagoon, then after a day at the water parks, back to the room and then back in to the pool till 11pm. At one point I had to force the kids to go to the parks that didn't involve water. Once there, Hannah spotted a massive slide and immediately wanted to go down it. I agreed, the only problem was that I had to put her on my shoulders and climb the steps of which I can assure you there were a lot. Immediately at the top, Hannah laid on the mat stomach first and went down the near vertical slide. My heart was in my mouth but I followed while Alice stood at the bottom afraid to try it.

As soon as we got to the bottom, we were back up again, this time all three of us. We loved it and must have spent a full afternoon on that slide, all three of us racing each other as we went down together.

The whole holiday was recorded on my personal

camcorder. One time Alice decided to do summersaults under water. I was at a distance recording both of them. Hannah shouted me to record, I did and as Alice came back up, her face was bleeding. She had cracked her tooth and bit her lip causing it to bleed. Even though she was panicking, I kept rolling and watched how sisterly love kicked in as Hannah took care of Alice for once. The tables had been turned. It was a small cut but nothing major. Alice was okay after we had a quick visit to the medical centre, and an ice cream sorted the problem moments later.

One of the lasting memories I had was visiting a theme park off the 192 highway. I had deliberately tried to keep away from it, knowing the Hannah would want to go on that catapult. By chance, we ended up walking by the ride and Hannah was asking to go on it. We had to do it, she saw no danger. She was asked to stand against a height chart and was literally one inch over the height mark, so that was it we had to go on it, and for fun I was going to pay for the recording of the whole episode. We were strapped in and ready to go. This was when I started to panic. What if she slipped out? Was she too small? I was assured everything would be okay, and it was. After getting home and showing Nicola the video, she wasn't too happy but chuckled at the fact Hannah had done it. It was a video we all watched for years, especially much later at the hospital while Hannah was unwell. We loved to show all the staff to show just what a personality Hannah had, and how she was not afraid of anything.

While we were in Florida, we went to see the dolphins and killer whales perform. Alice would sit on the back row of the arena, the driest place available, completely out of the splash zone. Personally I would have sat with her but no, Hannah wanted to sit right in the splash zone where the whale would drench us. We visited this attraction four times in a row and we were drenched each day, but dried quickly due to the heat.

The best thing about the holiday for me was to just watch the kids' faces while we did something different every day (if we weren't in the pool). We loved feeding the dolphins, and the kids wanted to do this as much as they could, and the highlight of the holiday was swimming with the dolphins. I had deliberately organised this for the second from last day so they could look forward to it.

Our dolphin was trained to roll over and lay on its back in the water, and while doing this it had a wee. Hannah and Alice laughed and it was something Hannah would mention for years. I placed the camcorder on the wheelchair, covered it with a towel and pressed record. It recorded the whole time we swam with the dolphins.

The day was split in to two. We swam with dolphins in the morning, and looked forward to swimming in a large pool with the tropical fish in the afternoon. The year before I had been to Australia and the Great Barrier Reef and fed the fish by hand by basically holding bread in the water. The fish would come up in packs and feed from your hand so I knew the kids would love this and have another memory to keep. Problem was, there was a sign saying 'Do not feed the fish'. I didn't see how a little could do any harm, so at lunchtime I said to the kids, "Keep the bread buns and hide them as we go in the water with all the fish. You're going to experience a lovely surprise but don't let anyone see what we are doing."

As we stepped into the water, I found a quiet place and placed a bread bun under the water. Immediately shoals of fish surrounded all three of us, and began fighting to eat the bread. I told the kids to do what I was doing with the bread, and they did. To see their faces was amazing as the fish that both Hannah and Alice had been previously trying to get near in the massive pool were now eating from their hands.

I could write so much about the holiday. It was fun the whole time we were there. It wasn't always easy. I was the only adult and I had two kids with me. Of course they squabbled at times, especially when we were in the car, and one time I got lost and ended up at the same toll station four times in the space of an hour, with no one to help me look at a map. I was stressed looking after them alone but I knew we'd have so many memories to talk about in the future it was worth being a little stressed.

Overall the holiday was the happiest time of my life. I knew that one day soon Hannah would leave us but I hoped and prayed I would be wrong. All three of us had the time of our lives. As we travelled back on the plane, I looked at them both asleep, worn out, and I knew as a father I'd given them memories that would last a lifetime.

CHAPTER 7

Back To The RVI…
October 2004

It wasn't long after the trip to Florida that Hannah started to become unwell again, around late August, early September 2004. It had been nearly five years since she looked this way, and it had signs of a renal issue. She was weak and a different colour. Nicola called me to come and see her as she was worried. Hannah just wanted to rest on her mam, and didn't care that I had popped round to see them. This was serious. I knew immediately that she needed to be at the hospital. Within an hour or two the staff at JCUH had confirmed that Hannah's blood results showed there was an abnormality.

We were off again on the way to Newcastle. It was a renal issue just as I had suspected. Hannah knew she was unwell and as she was being wheeled to the ambulance through the hospital, she said something to her mam, a short sentence that will stay with me forever. She looked up to her mam and said, "Mam, am I going to die?" She was six years old. How could she be thinking these thoughts? I had to ask Nicola to repeat what she had said, hoping I'd misheard. Nicola just shook her head.

Once again we were told the worst that could happen.

It was five years after Hannah's first kidney failure. For some reason they had stopped working correctly and had failed again, but this time a blood transfusion was not the answer. It was tried but was unsuccessful, therefore the alternative was plasma exchange. This had been mentioned briefly in 1999, five years earlier. It was a sort of dialysis where plasma, the liquid part of your blood, is replaced with a donor or replacement plasma, and would involve an operation to insert tubes (arterial line) into her body which meant sedation.

On the day of the operation, I was at home. I had been at work and picked Alice up from school. Work was being good to me and allowing late starts and early finishes, whether it was to drive to the hospital, or take Alice to school or pick her up. I had been in contact with Nicola on and off the whole day to ask about the operation. I finally heard it had been a success and Hannah was out of theatre and asleep.

Janine and me had made tea for us all and I explained to Alice it had all gone well. At around five o clock the phone rang. It was Hannah. She spoke softly and sounded drowsy and we told each other how much we loved each other, then she asked me to come up. I knew I had to even if it would be an hour and a half due to the traffic. I arrived at the hospital and walked into ward seven at Newcastle RVI around six thirty. Hannah was two beds down on the right hand side of the ward. She turned her head to me and smiled. I was shocked that she was still wearing in the gown which had blood on from the operation, and at that moment I have never in my life felt so much sorrow for someone. It was heartbreaking to see.

I grabbed her gently and hugged her tight then remember in the background a radio playing. In the distance you could hear the Coldplay song, 'I Will Fix You'. Whether it was fate or not, I sang the song to her quietly, and the look and smile she gave me told me she knew I would try no matter what was thrown our way.

Whilst at the RVI, Hannah was diagnosed with another illness called Haemolytic Uremic Syndrome (HUS). Everything was once again touch and go. Why did this keep happening? What was the cause? There was never an answer. It was so frustrating as Hannah was more aware now and was sick to death, and we couldn't give her an answer. When it was my turn to look after Hannah, we would try and have as much fun as we could under the circumstances. As the days went by, she was slowly getting better and it was quite warm outside so as it was just me and Hannah I decided to ask if we could nip out for a walk. The consultants deliberated and between them said it was okay.

Now given the fact where we were geographically positioned in the centre of the city, the majority of people would have gone and done some shopping, but no, not us. We went the opposite way and somehow by chance found a shelter for cats and dogs. Now this was more than a play area for Hannah, it was her idea of fun. We asked if we could just come round and look. Hannah was in her wheelchair but managed to project herself out and drum up enough energy to get around the place without any problems when the owners agreed. We spent a full afternoon watching the cats with their kittens, the dogs and their pups, and she loved it. Because it was animals, Hannah was in her element. She didn't want to leave but eventually, due to the medication she was on, it was time to go back and take another dose. I promised we would go there again when it was my turn to come up next.

I went home and Nicola took over. I had work the next day so it was back to Redcar to spend the night at home with Janine and then carry out a day's work, all the time trying to spend time with Alice too.

Alice would always want to come up to the hospital at weekends, and sometimes the odd day when she would be missing Hannah so much that a day off school was allowed. Crawford House, the building in the hospital grounds at Newcastle RVI for parents only, was used as a chance to get away from the hospital. It was a fully equipped house with rooms for all parents of children who were ill, a way of trying to bring a bit of normality and letting families spend some time together. Parents would label their food and place it in the fridge, or cupboards to prevent it being used by other parents. Anyone who didn't follow these rules were swiftly dealt with by the lady who ran the house. She was a lovely woman but would take no nonsense off parents not following the rules.

Hannah was slowly getting better so when I was up

at the hospital, Nicola would take Alice for the day and spend time away from the hospital either taking her to school or picking her up from school. We had to try and make things as normal as possible for Alice.

I did some investigating and found a park with animals around two miles from the hospital. Myself and Hannah got in the car and off we went. It was a lovely sunny day so we knew it would be ideal. Hannah was excited as I pushed her around in the wheelchair. She was much more mobile now so loved the chance to go in different directions to give her a chance to be out of the hospital and see as much of the park as she could, but more importantly spend time with the animals.

There was a small pony in a large enclosed area. We walked over to it and there were lots of parents there with children either stroking the head and nose or feeding it carrots. I had an idea. I said to Hannah, "Watch this", as the pony walked by the fence rubbing the side of its stomach. It was evident it needed to scratch its side, so quickly as it was passing, I rubbed its back so hard it stopped dead in its tracks and wouldn't move.

I had the pony there where I wanted it. It didn't want to be anywhere else. Hannah was up stroking it and loved the fact it was with us. Around the pen there were at least twenty sets of parents with children, all standing holding carrots and making noises to gain its attention to have it come near them. But it was no good. As I continued to rub the back of the pony as hard as I could, it just didn't want to move.

Two days later we returned to the park. As soon as the pony spotted us, it ran the full length of the pen to come to us. The parents and children couldn't believe it and asked if we were the owners. Hannah told a little white lie and said it was hers. She was in the zone and in her head it was her pony. Hannah loved it and over the years she would tell people the story of how the pony loved her so much it would run up to her.

We would disappear from the ward whenever we could to go to the park and see the pony and other animals. Hannah would walk up to people in the park sat picnicking, and if they happened to have a dog she would ask if she could sit and stroke it. It was odd while I stood there waiting for her to complete the cycle as she went round to everyone who had a dog, but this was Hannah the animal lover.

Back at the hospital one night, it was my turn to stay with Hannah and sleep by the side of her bed. She was close to coming home so her sense of humour was back with a vengeance, funny little girl. Every night, regardless, a nurse would call in to the room every couple of hours to check on her while a parent slept alongside her in a separate bed. On this specific night as the nurse came in, I got up to go to the toilet. As I returned, the nurse had put on the lights in the room and was all flustered with another nurse by her side, laughing. Immediately I knew it was okay as the second nurse was in fits of laughter yet the nurse who'd checked on Hannah was in a bit of a state.

I asked what had happened and was told the by the first nurse that as she leant over to take Hannah's observations, she woke and looked at the nurse with a panicky-looking serious face, then started gasping for breath for a second or two, then went stiff, stared at the nurse holding out her arm for help, then let out a sigh, dropped her arm, closed her eyes and went limp. The nurse thought she had died, quickly pressed the emergency button for help and turned on the lights.

I had to tell Hannah it may have been funny in her eyes but she shouldn't do that in the hospital as there were sick children in there. She understood but gave me that smirk, knowing I was telling her because the nurse in shock was standing behind me. I gave her a wink and smile without the nurse seeing. Hannah knew we would have a laugh about it when we left the hospital, which was drawing closer and closer.

Hannah was discharged from the hospital around October 2004. Beneath her clothes, she had tubes inserted in her chest for the plasma exchange which would start off three times a week for now. She also had a tube for liquid only. What next? How much more could my little girl take?

CHAPTER 8

Adventures, Mishaps And A Love Of Animals…
October 2004 – December 9th 2005

It was around this time we bought a puppy. It was a long legged Jack Russell terrier. Each of the three kids wrote a name on a piece of paper and folded it up, then all three sat patiently while me and Janine looked at the names. Two had picked the same name so the dog was to be called Patch, Sean and Hannah's choice.

Alice wasn't a big dog lover. She was more for cats. Unfortunately I was allergic to these so it would have to be a dog. Years later when Hannah became ill and came home, I would go round to see her at her mam's house. Nicola had cats and I would be sneezing for the full time I was round there.

Patch took some time to house train but what struck us all was the way he took to Hannah and she took to him. On one occasion, Janine heard banging and crashing downstairs and came down to see what was going on. As she walked into the kitchen, Patch came flying across the kitchen floor, to then get up and go running back to Hannah. Janine asked Hannah what she was doing to which Hannah replied, "Watch this, Janine, Patch loves it." Hannah would pick up Patch by his collar and spin round until he was three feet in the air spinning with her. As she did this to pick up speed, she would let go and Patch would fly through the air for around five feet. As gravity took hold, he would drop just before he reached the table and chairs and then crash in to them. He was about twelve weeks old at this time but he loved it and would keep coming back for more and more.

As time went by, they become inseparable. Every time I picked up the kids from their mam's house and we pulled on to the drive, Patch would hear Hannah's voice from behind the gate and go crazy, running from the side of the house, round to the back door, jumping up and down at the French doors at the back of the house waiting for Hannah to come through the house to see him. Hannah would come in, take off her shoes, then her splints that aided her walking, then off came the socks, trousers and there she was in her vest and knickers playing with Patch.

We decided to take a holiday to a caravan park at Primrose Valley during this time and it was to be our very first and, unfortunately, last holiday where all five of us would be together. Alice was feeling under the weather at the time with a bug so it was hit and miss whether she would come but Alice being Alice, nothing would stop her and off we went.

Looking back it was a great break, only four nights, cramped in the caravan but good fun. We went on the beach for the day as the weather was great, and in the clubhouse on the night. While me and Sean just sat, Alice, Hannah and Janine would be up dancing.

We went swimming the next day and Hannah, Alice and Sean spent an hour going down the slide, while Hannah decided to throw her goggles down to the slide to see what happened, only to find them disappear into the vent system, which I did warn her about.

That day we went back for lunch and we were all chilling, me and Janine making lunch, Alice and Sean sat watching TV and also Hannah or so I thought. Then suddenly I could hear a voice in the distance. It was Hannah's voice crying and pleading with me to help her. I shot round to notice Hannah wasn't there. Where was she? I said to Sean and Alice, "Where is Hannah?" but they both shrugged their shoulders, engrossed in the programme on TV.

By now I'm panicking. I can hear her voice, she's upset and calling me. She's been snatched but she's close, I'm thinking and I'm shouting back, "Hannah, keep calling me. I can hear you! I'm coming to get you." I had visions she had been snatched and was in a neighbouring caravan. Hannah could be so naïve and would go off with anyone especially if they had said they had puppies, that was it. No matter how many times I had warned her, if an animal was mentioned in the conversation she was off.

It was then that I realised her voice was coming from the car. The boot, in fact. I opened it and she leapt out and hugged me so tight. She had never been so scared in her life and here was her dad to the rescue. Immediately I turned to Alice and Sean, standing in the doorway, looking panicked, and I said to them, "You locked her in the boot? How could you do this?"

They looked at each other and said, "It was nothing to do with us. We didn't do it!"

I turned to Hannah as she was calming down. She was still clinging to me, visibly shaken. I asked her again what had happened and the reply was a classic to which we all laugh still when talking about that day.

"Well dad," she said, "I was just standing near the boot of the car and happened to look inside, and as I was looking, the wind blew me in and at the same time the boot closed."

It was a classic Hannah white lie to cover a prank. She must have opened the boot, got inside, pulled down the boot and immediately panicked. We all knew what she had done but she still stuck to the same story for years.

We would often go for early morning walks with Patch and the kids or just go out for the day. Another lasting memory was the day me, Alice, Sean, Hannah and Patch went to Moorsholm Woods and Lingdale Quarry. Due to the terrain, I knew Hannah would spend the majority of the day on my shoulders as she had done for years when it became difficult for her to walk with her splints, but I wasn't worried. She enjoyed being up there, ruffling my hair after I had put wax or gel on it. I got used to it.

So off we set to Moorsholm Woods from Redcar. I parked the car and knew I would have my hands full for the day with all three and the dog. Janine was at work so couldn't come so it was up to me. We walked to the woods, me holding Hannah's hand to prevent her falling over the divots in the ground, then if I wasn't holding her hand, it was Alice or Sean.

I showed them the areas I spent years playing as a kid. It was a red hot day so I had smothered them all in sun cream as they walked with shorts on and no tops. It was then that Hannah saw a dried cow pat and asked me what it was as she put her foot on it. I told her not to stand on it as it was cow poo, but too late, her shoe was covered, and to make it worse there was no water to clean it and the flies immediately were attracted to this so they began swarming around her foot. Just then Patch decided to run off and chase the cows. As there was young within the herd, they immediately began chasing Patch, who in turn was running back to us in this large field. Unfortunately we were in the middle and had to make it to a fence two hundred yards away. I said to the kids to run to the fence, everyman for himself, and started laughing to stop the kids panicking. They ran and I picked up Hannah as I knew it was impossible for her to run. Up she went on to my shoulders, but then it dawned on me as we started running, her feet were bouncing up and down and I was getting her shoe in my face every step I took. I was getting a mouthful of cow shit, so I was running, making sure the kids got to the fence in time and also retching due to the cow shit. It was funny looking back.

On another occasion I was working for the council one

Saturday at a carnival in town. The kids were with their nana and granddad along with Charlie, their cousin.

I came round the park and from a distance I saw Alice, Hannah and Charlie, who in turn saw me. They all started running to me. As Hannah had splints she could never run and just walked fast but it was still at a slow pace. I could see that, as Alice and Charlie were getting close, Hannah was becoming distressed. She was wanting to get to me at the same time as both Alice and Charlie did. Unfortunately I knew that by the time they got to me we would be waiting another forty seconds to a minute for Hannah to reach us. She would arrive frustrated and angry and possibly start crying, and again I would hear the words from her mouth as I had so many times before, "These stupid legs, I'm sick they don't work like everyone else." So what did I do? I ran to them, passed both Alice and Charlie and told them to follow me. We all came together at the same time and Hannah was over the moon. No one reached me first, we all met together and we hugged. It was a small gesture but we all knew it would mean the world to Hannah. For once she wasn't last.

Later that same year I was back living in Redcar and I received a call from Nicola. She was panicking and said, "Hannah is ill. She needs to go to the hospital. Can you come round?" It was the call I always dreaded.

Earlier that day Hannah had been to Newcastle for her plasma exchange and had been hooked up to the dialysis type machine for four hours. My immediate reaction was that she'd had a possible reaction to her treatment.

I slammed the phone down and went. Alice was packing her bag to stay at nana's house and Nicola was on the phone to the doctors. I asked Alice where Hannah was to be told she was sitting on the toilet with a bowl as she was being sick and also having problems with diarrhoea. As I walked in to the toilet to speak to Hannah I knew I had to assess the situation and try and establish why this had happened so suddenly, something must have triggered this, and I knew the only person who could help at this point was Hannah.

I asked her what she'd been doing, to which she replied, "I've been on Aunty Kendra's trampoline all day with Alice and Charlie."

"All afternoon?" I said. "It's been red hot today. Have you had plenty of drinks?"

"No," she said. "But I've had four and a half choc ices."

I kissed her on the forehead, told her I loved her and went to take the phone off Nicola. I explained to the doctor what Hannah had just told me and, as I thought, he explained the dangers of allowing Hannah to be so active after plasma exchange.

I told Alice to empty her bag and that Hannah would be okay, and after that night, we would always have a laugh about the choc ices for a long time after, although at the time it wasn't funny for Hannah.

As time went on Nicola decided to take Hannah out of the school in Redcar and allow her to go to a school called

Pennyman at Ormesby, Teesside, a school that catered for children with disabilities but was still a mainstream school. Hannah loved it. A bus would pick her up on a morning and take her home again on a night, dropping off and picking up other children along the way.

On one occasion I had the pleasure of taking Hannah to school at Pennyman due to her sleeping in. We actually beat her bus that day and she said to me, "Dad, stand here with me. I will take Zoe to her class and then I'll show you my friends." I was a bit confused but stood in the background. The bus back doors were open. Bruce, the driver, lowered Zoe down the ramp of the tail gate and looked at Hannah. She knew it was safe to walk over and that's when I figured this must be their routine every day. Bruce got Zoe off the bus and Hannah took her to the classroom. Typical Hannah, always helping out.

Hannah then told me to follow her while she pushed Zoe to her classroom in her wheelchair, applied the brakes, said goodbye to Zoe and walked off. She grabbed my hand and led me to her classroom where introduced me to her friends. Most were able bodied, but then I recognised a girl who immediately recognised me. She had been in hospital as a baby when Hannah was first there and over the years became a regular. She would always say hello through her tracheostomy and sign language to me. Although I didn't know sign language, I would always reply some way she knew, and now years later she was with Hannah in the same class.

As I've said, Hannah was animal crazy. She wanted to be a vet when she was older. That's the dream and vision she had. I had never met anyone who would want to be with animals and speak to animals as much as her when she met them. On one occasion we visited Janine's mam's house, it was the first time Hannah and Alice had been there, they had a cat that was around sixteen years old. It had been feral when Janine's dad Harry had taken it from the yard he worked at some years before. Only one or two people had ever stroked it or been near it, Janine when she was younger and Harry once or twice.

As we all entered the house Hannah spotted the cat and made a bee line for it. As it lay in the corner of the room, it was evident it would claw or attack her or run if she got any closer. She sensed this and over the next hour as we all spoke in the room, Hannah would concentrate only on the cat. It was as if she had shut everyone out and was talking to the cat in her own little world. It was looking at her and she was concentrating on getting closer. Harry had said she wouldn't get anywhere near the cat but she ignored him. All the time Hannah was concentrating on the cat, Alice sat on my knee as she would whenever we were in a place she wasn't sure of or hadn't been before.

Hannah was moving literally a centimetre a minute to get close to the cat. As she got close and it hadn't moved, Harry was a bit worried and commented. I said she would be okay. I wasn't concerned. Before we knew it, the cat had stood up and walked to Hannah and laid on her knee.

She stroked it and spoke to it for the next hour. Harry and Janine's mum Veronica were dumbfounded. They couldn't believe what they were seeing. This was the gift Hannah had, a special gift which is very rarely seen in a six year old child.

One night when Hannah was sleeping at my house, I asked if she would like to get up really early with me and take Patch up to Dunsdale Woods where we could watch Patch chasing rabbits. Hannah immediately said yes as if I had just offered her a holiday at a theme park.

I woke her at six thirty in the morning, helped her get dressed, put on her splints and shoes, then we had breakfast and put on our coats, put Patch in the car and off we went. It was still slightly dark when we reached the woods. It was then that I realised the sun would be coming up at some point very soon, so I carried Hannah up a steep incline through the woods so we could watch the sun come up.

Patch was too busy. He had disappeared. It was common for him to do this and turn up when I whistled him, so I wasn't concerned, he was hunting as a working terrier would.

I placed Hannah down as we had reached the top of the incline and stood by her side, holding her hand. As we did this, the sun was slowly coming up.

Hannah turned to me and said, "Wow, dad, isn't this so beautiful?"

I turned to her and knelt down beside her and replied,

"Yes, it's so beautiful, and there aren't many people your age who have ever seen this. They will see the sun going down but not coming up. So remember this."

Just then Patch came running up, telling us he had just chased something, I knew by the way he was reacting, so we went to see what he was telling us, and it was then that he took us to an area where he had found a badger sett and was on the scent. I was concerned he would go down a hole and get trapped, so we set off down the incline to the path at the bottom. It was about one hundred metres away down so we set off with Patch behind us. When we reached the bottom, I turned and noticed Patch wasn't there so I asked Hannah to wait and I set off back up the hill.

I reached the top in no time, and then began to whistle Patch. Luckily I saw him before he went down the badger hole. It was difficult to get him to come to me but in the end he did. My concern now was Hannah alone on a path in the woods. I shouted Hannah as I couldn't see her through the trees, and was relieved that she shouted back. I told her I was coming, and me and Patch started to run down the incline, then I lost my step, tripped and began falling. I was going too fast. I had just got back up on to my feet while still travelling at speed, and I could see Hannah and knew she could see me, and just then there was a branch that I knew I had to grab to slow me down. I grabbed it at the last minute, but it was no good, it was rotten and snapped as soon as I reached for it and gripped it. I landed on the path in a heap. Hannah was laughing hysterically and Patch was now jumping all over me, thinking it was a game.

I got up and brushed myself down while laughing myself. No injuries so that was good, then me and Hannah had a conversation that has lasted so long in my mind and was so funny at the time.

"Were you okay while I was up there?" I asked.

"Yes," she said. "Did you hear them pheasants in the bushes earlier? I was talking to them. The baby chicks came out from the bushes, and they were talking to me for ages, but then their mam came out and said, 'Come on, chicks, get on my back, you can't talk to her. Can you not see that the dog will be here soon? He's up the hill with her dad. Get on my back and we'll all fly away.' Then as they got on her back and flew away, they were waving with their wings."

I laughed and said, "Don't be daft, pheasants don't talk," but then I realised this was Hannah. I agreed with her and said, "Oh yes, I did see them from the top of the hill. I saw them waving at you on their mother's back."

This was to be the last time me and Hannah were together alone prior to her losing her sight. If I had known that day what was round the corner within weeks, I would have stood on that hill with Hannah looking at the sun coming up and the rest of the countryside for the whole day.

As it is, the memory of that morning has stuck with me for so long, and at least we shared that moment together. When things were going bad, I would always remind myself of that morning. I would always remind Hannah of that morning over the years as she was laid in bed unable to see or move. We would talk about it and exaggerate it even more, making stories up of Hannah talking to even more animals. That morning is probably the most precious memory I have of Hannah. It was so special.

Unbeknown to everyone, the clock was ticking. Hannah would soon loose her sight. It was December 9th 2005. I had spoken to both Alice and Hannah that day after they came back from school. They weren't to sleep that night as they were going to the pictures with their mam to watch The Lion, the Witch and the Wardrobe. They were excited so I told them they could sleep another time and to have a good time. I needed to go to the shop so I said I would say hello when I passed by.

I called at the shop and drove back past their house. I knocked on the door and it was opened by Nicola. I stood and at the entrance to the door and Hannah was in the kitchen fifteen feet away. She saw me and ran in her own little way as fast as her legs would take her, calling me as she came. She hugged me and I hugged her back. We spoke and I told her to enjoy herself. She gave me a kiss on my cheek and I told her I loved her. It was the last time Hannah would ever see me again. That night in the early hours of the morning, her sight would be taken from her without warning.

The stroke of midnight 2000… both Hannah and Alice stayed up for the new century.

Hannah in Florida kissing the dolphin. I'm out of sight but I'm holding her up.

67

Hannah enjoying the beach in Ibiza.

Hannah and Alice meet Mickey Mouse. Alice has her autograph book ready.

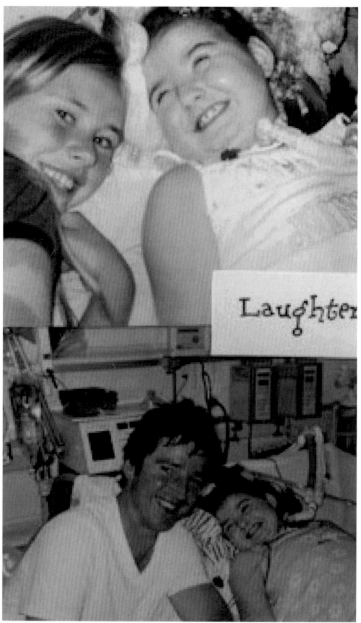

Laughter

Fun time with Alice and Hannah at Newcastle General, preparing for the move to JCUH.

CHAPTER 9

In And Out Of Hospital, Waiting For The Bombshell…
10th December 2005 Onwards

On the 10th December, with Hannah unable to see and all of us in a state of panic, we arrived at Newcastle RVI and were quickly processed through the system. Hannah had been a regular there over the last few months having her plasma exchange so they knew her well. Our objective was to find a consultant in neurology who we considered the best in his field to help us out immediately to try and fix Hannah's sight problem. We were hoping on a miracle answer.

The day was a complete blur as both me and Nicola spoke to what seemed like every consultant available. They would question us on the previous day's events leading up to Hannah losing her sight, and Hannah would just be curled up in a ball either on the bed she had been allocated, or in her mam's arms or mine.

An MRI scan was eventually planned that night to assess what was going on from a neurological perspective. Due to it being a Saturday, it seemed to take forever, however around 10pm Hannah was asked to lie down as still as she could as the consultants explained what was happening. Music was played so she could relax more as she had to lie there for what seemed like an eternity as the machine slowly slid her through the scanner. The consultants stood in a glass room peering through a window at the scanner and then looking down at the monitors. They were establishing what damage was done, or what could be repaired.

I stood against a wall in the room, looking at the consultants and Hannah, and trying to pick up on a sign from the consultants, a smile as if to say, "Oh yes, this has happened, it's a common infection, we will give her medication and she will be fixed." I spotted nothing.

Once the MRI scan was complete, they came out of the glass room with heads down, no eye contact with either me or Nicola, took Hannah from the machine as carefully as they could and placed her back on the hospital bed to be wheeled away back to the ward. As the nurses wheeled Hannah back to the ward, the consultant who had been in charge looked directly at Nicola, placed a hand on her shoulder and walked away. That gesture, that movement and the fact he said nothing said everything we wanted to know. This was going to be a major problem for Hannah.

We were given some basic information from another consultant when we arrived back on the ward which included that the scan had showed that Hannah's optic chiasm had swollen severely which prevented signals being permitted from her brain to allow her to see. We would be given more answers the next day.

I drove home that night around midnight, while Nicola stayed with Hannah. It was probably one of the most deflating journeys I was to take. Over the coming days and weeks we would speak to many consultants, while Hannah would stay as an inpatient, only this time she was to be transferred to Newcastle General, as the RVI was not the most practical hospital for Hannah's needs.

Hannah was eventually discharged to be home for Christmas. She didn't want to leave her mam's side, but with the reassurance of Alice by her side, she came to my house on Christmas Day. Alice and Sean opened their presents, while me, Janine, Alice and Sean explained what Hannah's presents were. She wasn't impressed and was just sad. I left the room and went upstairs, locked the bathroom door and cried. I felt hopeless and useless at the same time. After ten minutes, I composed myself so as to not let anyone know why I had disappeared, and tried to carry on the day as normally as I could.

Although it was difficult for everyone involved, more so Hannah, we had to do the best we could. The majority of the time Hannah would stay at her mam's. She had many medicines which made her gain weight and also made her need the toilet constantly. She was so confused with this new way of life. She wanted nobody but her mam. Trust with everyone else went out of the window.

When Nicola needed a break, I forced her to let me help and have Hannah at my house for a night here and there. Hannah came reluctantly but settled in the end. Patch would hear her voice and he would dive all over her. Hannah was so frustrated that she couldn't see him. It was hard for all of us. But as the months went by,

Hannah came round more often. On one occasion, as me and Hannah were in the front room, we could hear kids playing out the front. Alice and Sean were two of them, and Hannah could hear them. She turned in my direction and told me she wished she could play outside. That was it. I put on my coat and then put on Hannah's as it was windy. As we went outside, I held Hannah's hand and signalled to Alice and Sean to let them know we were coming out to play with them. With the wind being so strong, we held plastic bags and let the wind blow them. Hannah loved it. It was one of the first times she had laughed for a while.

That same night we all went to the shop. We were going to be real quick as the kids just wanted sweets, so it was easier for Hannah to sit and wait in the car. We quickly ran in, I gave Alice and Sean the money and went back to Hannah. As I approached the car, Hannah was sitting, looking ahead with her hands in front of her, looking as if she was praying. I opened the door not to startle Hannah and asked if she was okay. What she said next to me struck me to the core.

"I was praying to God and Jesus," she said, "to ask them if they can give me my sight back because I don't like not being able to see no more."

I didn't know what to say. What could I say? I was in denial, thinking it would come back, but deep down I knew it wouldn't. Alice and Sean got back in the car, and we drove back to the house. I didn't say anything to anyone about what Hannah had said, but as a father I was defeated. But I had no choice but to continue being as positive as I could.

Before Hannah lost her sight we would go horse riding. Hannah and Alice would have a horse each and my friend's wife would hold one horse and walk with it, I would hold the other and we would walk a route of about three miles. I asked if it would be possible if we could do it again after Hannah lost her sight, as she was becoming more trusting with me. That day my friend Martin, his wife Sheena and their two daughters, who were talented horse riders, were waiting for us when we arrived. Hannah knew the horses' names from a few months back, pre-sight loss, and asked to ride Rosey.

This time was different. We had to have one person on one side and one on the other. We helped Hannah get on the horse, then Alice jumped on the one behind. It was a happy time moving forward, as Hannah was back doing things she liked. Martin's two daughters were talking to Hannah and Alice the whole time, reassuring Hannah and explaining where we were during the ride so Hannah could relate to the environment she had previously seen on the past rides through the countryside. Martin's two girls were brilliant. Although they were young, they knew how difficult the whole episode was for us all that day.

Another visit to Great Ormond Street (GOS) was looming due to Hannah's sudden loss of sight and it arrived late March, early April 2006. Nicola would take her down and between me and Nicola's mam we would look after Alice.

Two days later both myself and Alice went down to GOS to see Hannah. For anyone who has never been, this place is unbelievable. The hospital is the best in the world. It's heartbreaking to see the pain and anguish etched on the faces of the parents with sick children, but more importantly to see the poor children who have to go there for treatment is one of the most heartbreaking experiences I have ever witnessed. After a good day together, it was time to go home again, and me and Alice travelled back on the train. Around this time drama was a passion of Alice's so I spent the time on the way back helping her with her lines for the lead part, she would be playing as Alice in Alice in Wonderland.

Hannah was soon home again but only two weeks after that GOS visit, she became unwell, a sign of infection brewing. We decided that she needed to go to the hospital so Nicola drove her there around 6pm that night and went through the usual protocol of taking blood samples and waiting for results. At that point Nicola was continuously explaining the signs were exactly the same as episodes in 1998 and 2002 in which Hannah slowly lost her mobility. I was at home and Alice was sleeping over that night. She could see I was stressed, on and off the phone, establishing what was going on. She went to bed around 9pm as it was school the next day. I told her a bedtime story and reassured her all would be okay with Hannah. I called the hospital around 10.30pm to be told Hannah was rapidly becoming worse. That was it. I had to go up there and fast. I left Janine to look after Alice and if she woke in the night just to explain I was up at the hospital, but everything would be okay.

I arrived at the hospital around midnight and as I walked into the ward I was immediately asked to come into a side room by a nurse who had been waiting for me by the door. There waiting was the usual consultants, junior doctors, nurses and Nicola sitting in the room. It was evident it was serious as Nicola was upset with a nurse by her side providing tissues to wipe away the tears. My first thought was that I was too late, and Hannah had died while I was on the way up there. I was reassured she hadn't but there I was again, waiting for the possible answer to her sudden illness, knowing it would never come due to Hannah being a special case.

She needed to be transferred to the PICU at Newcastle General, as the resources to keep her alive were not available at the RVI. So off we went. I travelled behind the ambulance at 3am in the morning to another part of Newcastle. The ward was big and had lots going on. We were introduced to the staff who seemed professional, polite and caring, something I was now getting quite used to due to the amount of hospitals I had visited over the last few years.

Hannah was sedated. She was just being kept alive by machinery once again as we waited to find out answers.

This was a new environment where I knew nobody. I asked questions but received no answers.

A consultant approached Hannah's bed, nodded, said hello briefly then started issuing direct orders to the nurse in charge.

"Reduce the pressures," he said. "Let's see how she reacts. We need to see some movement. Keep me posted." Then he was off and on to the next bed. He was abrupt and direct. I knew I would like this fella and as time went on, I did. I remember him as Bob. For the life of me I can't remember his surname, but this fella was a good consultant.

Over the next few days, Hannah started to come round. Both me and Nicola were there along with Alice when she awoke. Nicola reassured her she was there and in return Hannah mouthed that she loved her mam with difficulty due to the tubes coming from her nose which went up and then back down past her vocal cords, a sight I had witnessed so many times before.

Around this time I was to have to take a back seat and allow Nicola to take care of Hannah. Hannah didn't want me near her, she couldn't understand why she had lost her sight previously, and now she had lost all mobility. She was too young to understand on the previous occasions her mobility had gone, but this time she knew and couldn't understand, but she had to vent her anger on somebody and that was me. If Nicola disappeared to the toilet, or for some fresh air, Hannah would cry and tell me to go away if I spoke to her. I knew by being patient I would win Hannah over again in time, like I had when she lost her sight on December 10th 2005. It had been weeks before she would allow me to take her anywhere, but I'd persevered and it had paid off in the end.

For weeks I would go to the hospital hoping for answers but nothing. It was a stressful time for all involved. After I had spent the day with Hannah, I would stay in a room provided which was annexed to the hospital and used for parents of children who were ill. Not as homely as Michael Crawford House at the RVI, but it was okay for me. I wouldn't be spending much time in there as the majority of the time I was on the ward, trying to comfort Hannah the best I could.

Hospital surroundings can become very stressful. I've witnessed many things happen over the years, children coming in to the PICU as an emergency, parents collapsing in a heap as their child is taken from them, rushed into PICU after being knocked over or having fallen from a derelict building, families not having the chance to prepare, say goodbye, looking at their faces as they are in total shock and denial that the doctor is explaining to them what is happening and how they can't do any more, listening to them squeal as all the energy is draining from them, trying to understand how the child they tucked into bed the night before and made breakfast for them that morning has gone forever.

One of the toughest incidents I witnessed at Newcastle General PICU was a step-father and mother refusing the biological father access to the room his son was dying in, because of the fact he hadn't seen his son for some time. On that day I felt so much for the father as he walked away, not having been given the chance to say goodbye to his son one last time. The two of them were probably the reason he hadn't seen his son because it was more trouble than it was worth trying to get access. The memory of that man walking away, broken, shoulders down, holding his head in his hands, begging the step-father to see his own child as the mother made no attempt to allow it, was dreadful. Luckily the doctors intervened and the man did get to spend some time with his son that day. I was so happy for him but sad at the same time as he was to say goodbye to his son forever as the boy died later that afternoon, thirteen and with his whole life ahead of him. It was a hard place to be.

During this time Hannah was headlining the local paper with her condition, but the newspaper articles were written in such a way that it looked like the only people who were involved with Hannah were Nicola's side of the family. I was a little bit shocked as I had just had time off to visit the hospital at Newcastle daily. I walked into the office one day to see three people standing around the newspaper while one read it out to the whole office, not expecting me to walk in as I didn't go up to the office a great deal. Ged looked at me and said, "You know, Andy, it doesn't mention you at all. It should but know this, everyone in this office knows how much you care, and how much you have done. Ignore the fact you're not mentioned. It will be old news tomorrow and the paper will be fish and chip paper." I laughed because the old fish and chip paper line was always used by everybody, even though old newspapers hadn't been used as fish and chip paper for the last ten years at least.

Over the following months, everyone throughout the council knew that Hannah was my daughter. I was asked everywhere I went how she was although people were kept up to date with the stories in the local newspaper. Frankly it was getting me down. I needed to move on. I didn't feel as sharp in my job and I was allowing things to slip. I couldn't concentrate. My head was all over. I took some more time off and then went back to work but it was a mistake. I had real trouble with a few people when I was at my weakest, going backwards and forwards to the hospital night and day. Luckily Ged had my back and made sure he took care of me, and for that I am grateful.

One afternoon we sat in the consultancy room waiting for a bombshell. Why else would we have both been called into the room together? It was Friday 26th June 2006. We had been there over six weeks. Hannah had not got any better. There was no movement from her. We had seen this before and eventually she had always ended up getting a lot of the mobility back. This time it was different. Hannah had undergone many tests and the results were not making sense.

During that time she had suddenly switched off and her body shut down twice, the alarms triggering and doctors rushing round to bring Hannah back to life. We were told after the second episode that Hannah would possibly leave us forever as the consultants had witnessed this happen and saw it as a sign the end was close. Alice was on holiday with her nana and granddad. We had to make contact and get her back as soon as possible. She arrived back the next day along with nana and granddad to say goodbye. Janine came up with Sean as we all prepared for the worst. Again, this was one of Hannah's many mysterious episodes and luckily she was not to spend her last weekend with us, again something that baffled the doctors.

But in the room that Friday in June, there were the three PICU consultants, junior doctors, nurses from the ward and the dialysis team from Newcastle RVI. It seemed a lot of people, around twelve in total. What was coming this time, I wondered? The meeting began with Bob the consultant explaining that tests had proven that Hannah's nerves were so badly damaged that she would never regain feeling from the neck down. She was paralysed for life from the neck down, and also blind. This was not happening. It was rubbish, I thought. Hannah had been here before and recovered. I wasn't ready to listen to this but did anyway.

Nicola started to cry and was being comforted by a nurse who would hand her tissues. By now, in my opinion, it was no use sitting there crying as I had experienced so much in the past. This was an opportunity to listen to the words of the consultants and doctors, time to absorb the information, analyse it and look back later, reflecting on the meeting and working out how life would be going forward for Hannah.

I listened as Bob explained that although this was a tragedy, a proposal had also been forwarded to allow a care package to be created to allow Hannah to eventually go home. This would take some time so he told us to be prepared for the long haul. As Hannah was stabilised, and had been for some time now, it was time to prepare for Hannah to go closer to home and be kept at JCUH in the PICU while the package was been built. This would make life easier for all. A one hundred mile round trip each time I visited Hannah was taking its toll.

Both myself and Nicola were over the moon for Hannah and Alice. Hannah arrived at JCUH after spending six months at Newcastle RVI. The staff seemed pleased to see her again and commented on how she had grown. It had been a while since she was last there. Some of the staff were still there from previously but a few new staff were there also. Hannah still needed to be hooked up to a ventilator and both me and Nicola had carried out some training in relation to clearing the build-up of phlegm which occasionally gathered in the trachea. I remember looking at the procedure being carried out some time previously and it looked difficult and horrendous to have to insert a tube down the trachea which then went so far into the throat. Once this was achieved, your thumb would be placed onto an air hole to allow the suction process to start. The staff could see that as parents we had now become more involved in this type of procedure.

In the background things were happening slowly with the package which involved Nicola's house being renovated to allow Hannah to come home. What transpired was that the kitchen would be altered. There wasn't much room but Nicola was happy with the set up. It wasn't until years later that the extension was deemed inadequate for such complex care and another extension would need to be carried out.

Staff came to us and went, mostly if they weren't ready or couldn't comprehend the magnitude of such care required and had to leave. It was frustrating as one after the other staff left after maybe a week, a month or even a day. I was never involved in the care side of things. At the initial meeting, I was asked what part I would play, how often I would be acting as a carer, it was obvious the purse string holders were trying to penny pinch to involve me. I explained I would play no part whatsoever in the clinical part regarding Hannah, and would not be acting as a carer to work all week and then carry out night shifts at my ex-partner's house. I would be Dad and Dad only and if Nicola had any sense she would do the same.

It was during this time Alice won the part of play Alice in Alice in Wonderland. It was shown at the Little Theatre in Middlesbrough in front of hundreds of people. Nicola wouldn't leave Hannah at the hospital and Hannah couldn't come to such events. It was heart breaking to watch Alice knowing she had so much going on, but as usual she performed brilliantly. I sat with Janine and Sean watching the show. I was so proud.

I have never ever forgotten the impact Hannah's illnesses had on Alice. Any other child would have grown up affected by the things she had seen and witnessed, but I could never in a million years have thought I could be as proud as I am for the way Alice always conducted herself.

I came home one day in the first six months of Hannah being at JCUH and just broke down in front of Janine. I said, "I don't know how Nicola copes with this but it's killing me. Hannah won't let me talk to her for at least an hour or two after her mam leaves, and her mam feels guilty for leaving which makes it worse for me because it's pointless me being there if her mam stays longer."

It was then that Janine said, "Why don't you make up stories but have Hannah in them? Talk about animals. You're good at talking rubbish so it will come better from you. Try it, you have nothing to lose."

I tried the next day. Slowly Hannah was allowing me to talk to her more. I made stories up about any and every animal in the world. In one story, baby foxes came in to a girl's house because they were lost. The girl looked after them, talked to them, fed them and played with them, then the mother and father fox came looking for the babies one day and went to attack the girl but the baby foxes jumped in and said that the girl was looking after them, so the mother didn't attack her but thanked her, then as the little girl stroked the baby foxes and said goodbye, the mother fox turned round and said thank you for looking after my babies, but I forgot to ask your name. The girl replied, "My name is Hannah Mae Dowson."

Within the stories, there were lots of twists and turns so each one lasted at least fifteen to twenty minutes. The aim of the story was for Hannah to think it was her. She was the little girl throughout the story. She had to be made to believe this, and the key to every story was for her to be allowed to say her own name right at the end. It worked brilliantly. I had an angle to get to talk to Hannah, but more importantly she was reacting to me in the right way. And it was amazing.

Time went by pretty slowly at JCUH. Hannah took another turn for the worse and it was around this time I decided to leave the council. I needed a challenge, and at the council I was constantly being asked about Hannah. I was seeing her nearly every night so that was my time with her, facing reality. At work I wanted to challenge myself and shut out the world just for a while. I applied for a role as an environmental manager, and over the next three years I had possibly one of the best jobs for learning and advancing that there could ever be. The job started out as environmental manager but ended up being more a role as operations manager as time went by.

I was instrumental in creating the documentation for the decommissioning of ships and offshore platforms. No day was the same. It took my mind off what was going on, and it was completely different from the council. The difference was, when I joined the private sector role, I made a point of not mentioning Hannah at all. I wanted to be measured on my performance, not having people feel sorry for me and everything my family was dealing with. For the first year I would go to the job and call in to the hospital two to three nights a week after work, and stay till I got Hannah off to sleep. Nicola would leave when I arrived as she had been there all day. On a weekend we would alternate. I would stay Saturday morning till late afternoon and then come back Sunday late afternoon till Sunday night. This went on for a year. At the same time, both me and Nicola were making sure Alice was looked after and taken to and from school. At the weekends Alice would call up to the hospital and either stay or leave with me or her mam.

In the whole of that year I would sit at the end of the bed and listen to Hannah cry and tell me to go away as she wanted her mam. She had done the same at Newcastle General for six months.

It was hard for me that Hannah didn't want me there. As soon as she heard my voice, she knew that was the sign her mam was leaving, whether it be immediately or after an hour or so. Nicola never wanted to leave and was always torn. Hannah wanted her mam and her mam only. Hannah had been my best friend whenever she was well.

She knew when she was with me it was an adventure. We would do something different. Now, she was hurting inside, and had so much mental pain, asking why she couldn't be doing those things again. The only way she could vent her anger were with words and those words were directed at me, as if I was to blame for her being ill.

I accepted it. It didn't bother me. Whatever she said, I would never leave her. I was her dad and I was here forever, no matter what the outcome. Many a dad would have walked away, but not this one. I know what it's like to not have a father there and there was no way any of my kids would experience it, even if me and Nicola were not together.

Before she went to sleep, she would be given medicine to relax her. This was the only time she would talk to me. I would sit at the end of the bed waiting until the sleepy meds were given, then I would have ten minutes talking to her as she was drifting off. I would stroke her face and tell her stories I would make up, and she would fall off to sleep, dreaming about the story I had told her, or she would listen to The Lion, the Witch and the Wardrobe, the last film she ever saw before losing her sight.

Those ten minutes were priceless. One occasion springs to mind how Hannah had tried her hardest to keep me away from her, and keep her mam staying longer. As I rang the buzzer to come into the ward, a nurse saw me through the screen and said, "Your dad's here, Hannah," to which Hannah replied, "I don't know why he keeps coming up to see me, he's not even my dad." This was

Hannah's sense of humour coming back slowly. I laughed when I was told this and Hannah laughed with me. It was the first sign in over a year that she had wanted to laugh with me. It was a sign of us getting back on track.

The staff were great at the PICU at JCUH. As time went by I got to know the new staff. There were some great characters and one such was Kerry Fox, wicked sense of humour and on my wavelength. I remember one time I had just got Hannah to sleep and in came a new carer from the new package currently being trained, one I had never met before.

She came in the ward like a tornado, walked up to Hannah's bed, bypassed me and said, "Hello Hannah, I'm one of your new carers and I'll be in here Monday looking after you," in a very loud voice. It startled Hannah who had just fallen asleep. She woke and quickly asked me who she was and why was she so loud. I turned to the woman and said, "I'm Hannah's dad. I've just got her to sleep and now you have woken her and startled her," to which the woman shot round and said sorry, only to knock Hannah's ventilator off the shelf. Immediately the alarms started to sound, Hannah couldn't get breaths, and the staff of the PICU had to jump up and sort the ventilator in record time. Hannah was now upset. She couldn't understand what had just happened. I reassured her, at the same time telling the new carer it would probably be best if she left now so I could sort Hannah out again.

After the commotion I looked over at the PICU team.

Kerry was sitting there, and we looked at each other and both started to laugh and couldn't stop. Hannah asked why I was laughing, and I said loudly, "If that woman had come in here on a motorbike, she would have not made as much mess and been as loud as she just has been." Kerry laughed more, I laughed but, more importantly, Hannah laughed.

During the time Hannah was in hospital, occasionally a lady would come and sing to her. It was evident Hannah just could not be bothered listening to her, and it was frustrating for Nicola who tried to get them to interact, but over time Hannah and the lady began to have a bond with each other. Then Jim the musician turned up, and every Thursday he would sing to Hannah, play instruments and bond with her. He was also to play a key part in introducing my singing skills to Hannah as he would play an acoustic version of The Jam's 'Town Called Malice'.

There were a lot of things going on in the background at JCUH. Hannah had missed a lot of school so occasionally a teacher would come in and speak to her and cover certain topics for a child at her age. Previously Hannah had been to mainstream school, where only slight modifications were required, a certain chair to enable her to sit in when the other children were sat cross-legged on the floor. Due to her having splints at the time to help her walk, she found it harder to get up on to her feet sat on her backside. Despite the length of time Hannah was in

JCUH, everything was ticking along but frustratingly, at a snail's pace. Eventually the package was ready, in a fashion, so around mid-July 2007, Hannah was to go home. With the welcome home banners at her house, Nicola had a vehicle to transport her as the day finally arrived.

CHAPTER 10

Struggling With Private Care Packages…
2007 – 2013

Although it was fantastic to think that your child that requires special care could come home, rather than spend a lifetime in hospital, we had a difficult time with the private packages that were arranged for us.

I have no doubt in my mind that the planning was done professionally and diligently, however, in reality the care was never right for us or Hannah.

Hannah had at least four different packages that failed for a variety of reasons, although one lasted quite some time because those three long term carers, Kerry, Claire and Laura, genuinely loved Hannah whilst working with her and had a very good relationship with her. Nicola also managed the care of this second package effectively with guidance from the three carers. They formed a good team but even still Hannah would be in and out of hospital occasionally where it would be required the care package work alongside the PICU nurses.

Every time Hannah's package failed in came the new package, and I would sit and listen to their commitment and values. It always sounded good but I had to listen to it no matter how many times I had heard it before. I would listen and use this initial meeting which showered us with commitment and quality care, to question them on at a later date when they were not managing effectively.

It frustrated me when Hannah had to go back in hospital as a care package failed again. And yes, both me and Nicola would argue with each other on the reasons and at times I would consider Nicola to blame, but that was my naivety on the level of care required for Hannah at that time. It was only later, after another package failed, that I realised that Hannah needed a better care system.

I have a lot of sympathy for the carers who came to look after Hannah. There were some fantastic people, but there were also some who struggled to comprehend the care needed.

I recall an occasion on the last package where the rota was day to day so I suggested a month to month. The care trust backed me up for once and agreed. It was a plan for April and May that was eventually produced, and I analysed the rota immediately, flabbergasted. Easter weekend – no carers. Both bank holiday weekends in May – again no carers. This meant only one thing – Hannah sitting in hospital on those important family weekends while the managers who'd produced the plan were sitting there smiling because they'd managed to cover three out of the eight weekends. I pointed this out immediately and reminded them of the commitment they'd made to both me and Nicola five months previous, which they seemed to have conveniently forgotten.

I'm aware that a lot of work was being put into the packages in the background and always appreciated the NHS Trust management listening to both Nicola and me when there was issues, but unfortunately it was always too late to act which then resulted in a whole new package being introduced, which in turn meant that Hannah would be back up to the PICU at JCUH. And yes, although she was to be looked after by the best care that could ever be supplied when she was there, and the care was brilliant at PICU, it wasn't the place for Hannah to be.

It wasn't always difficult when Hannah was at home with the care packages. She had become quite a celebrity in the area and everybody seemed to know her, or knew of her. Occasionally the village bobby would ride his police horse around Dormanstown, and he would bring the horse up to the double doors less than a metre or two from Hannah's bed. The horse would stick its head through the door where Nicola and Alice would feed the horse with apples. Hannah and Alice loved it.

One time Alice had a friend with a small pony. They brought the pony into the room where it stood while everyone described it to Hannah, and just then it decided to have a poo in Hannah's room. Hannah laughed and loved telling me all about it.

But trying to get a home care package right was turning out to be hard work. I have always been confident and forward, and when it came to Hannah I could switch on my management head. I've worked on some of the biggest projects around the world and always got results. These packages were simply to provide a care package, provide training for their staff and get them to interact with Hannah at the same time. Nicola knew the care side more than most due to the fact she had spent so long looking after Hannah, so between us we knew a lot, but I believed that some of the carers and management of the care package simply failed to realise that Hannah did not at any time ask to be put in this awful situation. Neither did Alice, or Nicola. We were all just trying to make the best of a horrible situation.

The whole time we were trying to get the care packages sorted, I was still working full time. I had been at my new job for well over a year before I finally told anyone about Hannah. Kelly was a girl who worked as the administration manager and had become a good friend. She had an excellent sense of humour and was someone I could confide in. As we were travelling to the sandwich shop one day, I told her everything about Hannah and that for the last year and a half I had been going to and from the hospital, calling there straight after work. She looked directly at me and burst into tears. She couldn't believe that I'd have kept it secret for so long. She asked questions for days even googling Hannah to read up on her. She promised to keep it secret which I appreciated, although as it was clear I could perform well in my job, I wasn't really bothered a great deal who knew now things had died down. Hannah was at home with a new package and I could relax a bit more. Life was starting to get better. I began taking courses paid for by the company to further my career and by the time I did leave I was qualified to be the HSE manager, logistics manager, and waste manager for all the sites.

During this time I was offered a role in Dubai, and even though it was tempting, I couldn't go and leave Hannah. She needed me and had only just got home. Even though I wasn't living there, I would pop round for an hour each night after work, tell her a story or two and then head home. As time progressed I felt another challenge was needed. I had outgrown the company and knew there were better opportunities on the market. A second opportunity arrived to work in Dubai in December 2009, and this time I felt it was right. Hannah's care package seemed stable, I had been there for the last four years since she lost her sight so I decided to go for it. I had some good qualifications and knew the position I was offered was the one. Janine was livid that I was leaving to go work in Dubai, Alice didn't want me to go, and Nicola complained on behalf of Hannah but my mind was made up. Was it the right choice? Was I running away and leaving everything behind? Only I know that, and it's me that has to live with my choices.

I regret going occasionally for missing out on Hannah and Alice, but Skype was a valuable tool to speak to everyone. I arrived and told no one of Hannah, the same as at my previous role. Over the months I began to get results where it counted for the company and became an asset. I streamlined operations and got the best out of the people to enable one operation that was previously producing 17,000 tons of stock a month to 164,000 tons a month as I trained the staff and managed them the way Ged had managed me all that time ago at the council. In return, I got just as much respect from the Indian workforce as I gave them. We were a great organisation to work for with some very good managers in other areas.

After a year, it was time to go home. I had promised Janine and the kids that was it. The whole time I was there I had not mentioned Hannah's illness to a soul. This was me. I never wanted sympathy ever, and by telling people the situation, how could they make things better? I dealt with it in my way, and over the last year it was by talking to Hannah, Alice and Janine on Skype daily, while counting down the days until I was home. Janine had been over a few times and Alice once. The problem was I had to wait three months before I could get home to see Hannah, and this wasn't good as I would only be home ten days or so maximum. My mind was made up. It was time to leave and I dropped the bombshell.

The company were shocked. I was seen as a vital asset going forward. They'd seen the results of my performance and saw me as a vital cog in the company going forward. It was at this point I gave the HR manager Rick my reason and actually told him to google Hannah as it would be easier to understand the real reason I was leaving.

By this time I was at home and was on a short leave. Rick called me with an offer to stay, as I had a residency visa and there was no way out of this, so we talked and negotiated. If I was to work six days a week and not five, after six weeks I would have accrued six days and could use them to go home. On top of this I would still have my 35 days holidays plus the country's usual holiday for Eid and national days, so at the end of every six weeks, I could go home for six days and use three to four of my holidays. At the time, this was a good deal. On top of this, the day I worked on a weekend would be at my apartment, so in other words I was still working five days and to top this off I was given a pay rise to allow flights home. I discussed all this with Janine, Alice and Nicola on behalf of Hannah and decided I would do it. I'd be coming home after six weeks now instead of between twelve and thirteen, which meant more time with Hannah.

I stayed in Dubai for another two years on this system and it worked well. At one point while working in Dubai, one of the lads got something in his eye which required a visit to the hospital. I took him in my car to one of the major hospitals in the UAE. After the eye specialist in the hospital had sorted him out, I mentioned Hannah and what had happened with her sight. The consultant was fascinated and wanted to see her notes. I couldn't get hold of these but I did have copies on a disc of her original MRI scan on the 10th December, the day she lost her sight.

I was really positive there could be something done to improve her eyesight and mobility after speaking to them, but it came to nothing.

I made my mind up it was time to come home. The company was winding down after the recession had hit and I was only working a maximum of three days a week. I was still on my rotation but I was bored. I was in a strong position to get work anywhere else but decided the offshore route was for me, working half the year on rotation of four weeks on and four weeks off. Given my skill set I reckoned I would easily find work in this industry. So I carried out the basic offshore courses and began looking.

As I was home more frequently, I could keep a close eye on developments, however come June 2012 it was evident that the current package was falling apart. I thought that if I could get home and have three months off, I could spend time with Hannah and at the same time help sort the new package to have Hannah at her house full time.

I arrived at the office, said hello to everyone and headed to Shaun's office on the 35th floor, overlooking Dubai Palm. This was some view, and as I stood looking out, I was mentally taking in everything to help me make up another story for Hannah using the surroundings when I spoke to her again.

Shaun showed me into his office and told me there'd been a change in plan. "I didn't want to tell you over the phone," he said, "but it's obvious we've not been getting work. The recession has hit us hard and Tim is having to lay us all off."

I had my notice letter in my back pocket but for some reason I kept quiet.

Shaun added, "We're going to be getting our apartments paid until the end of the term, all furniture and belongings will be shipped back and as a token of appreciation, anyone who has been with the company two years or more will get two months' salary. The thing is, Andy, we need you to stay until September. Assets are to be sold off and we need you to bring a site in Abu Dhabi up to Health and Safety standards. The staff need a lot of HSE Training. Would you be willing to stay till September?"

I couldn't believe what I was hearing. I'd been about to hand in my notice and by keeping my mouth shut for once I had just been offered two months wages, my tenancy on my apartment paid off and all my equipment shipped back. My immediate response was yes.

I knew that if everyone was being laid off it would be a skeleton crew of staff and I would be in a position to do what I was asked and nothing more, which meant possibly a day's work a week which allowed me to prepare for home which also meant when I was due home for my end of July trip home after six weeks I would stay home longer as I wouldn't be missed, and while I was home I could keep a close eye on the new package.

It all worked out and I arrived home 26th September 2012 with the intention of having three months off and returning back to work in a new environment in January 2013. I was to spend as much time with Hannah as I could, Alice was over the moon I was home which meant shopping trips and days out. Hannah was still in hospital, and we needed to find a new provider to run a new package from scratch. It would be a long time before Hannah would be home again. I was up at the hospital again every day and the trained staff who had crossed over from the previous package would be with me as we walked around. Hannah was becoming very well known by staff at the hospital.

After a month I was itching to start working again. No sooner had I started looking there was an opportunity working four weeks on and four off as a global Health, Safety & Environmental Trainer/Coach (HSE Trainer). I applied and within a week was at the main office in Romania for an interview and, after being shown the package, I accepted. It was a great opportunity as it meant that when I was home I would have lots of time to spend with Hannah at the hospital, or maybe even at my home with Hannah and the carers for an hour or two.

I set off to Trinidad around November 25th 2012 to join a rig. We were to navigate with the rig across the Atlantic Ocean. Little did I know that this date would be etched in my mind forever, as only two years later this was the very date I would lose Hannah in 2014.

CHAPTER 11

A New Package, The Pinkenators and Jessie J…
2014

It all came to a head one day when both me and Nicola were asked attend a meeting with the NHS Trust, some leading nurses, consultants, directors of the NHS trust, and the current package management team which meant a manager and area manager were in attendance. In total there must have been twenty people in a big room, all discussing Hannah's package and the problems, historical and present day.

I listened to all of the input from the others and then hit them with what they had all missed for years. If I remember correctly, my words finally sealed the fate of the private care packages and allowed everyone to finally see sense, that the private care packages involving individuals with a lack of training for Hannah's needs, along with managers with no clinical experience were to be finally done away with.

"What you all seem to miss," I said, "is staring you right in the face. If Hannah is at home with a care package and she becomes ill, she doesn't go to the doctors, or call up to the hospital to sit in the day unit to be examined, she goes directly to PICU. It's the only place she can go.

After PICU, she can't go anywhere else. In PICU she will have immediate care from nurses who have had to sit through years of study to become a qualified nurse. How can we say that a team managed by individuals with little or no clinical training, along with carers who were working in a completely different field previously before being employed to look after Hannah with a day or two's training, can come along and be expected to deliver the same kind of care the PICU do? It's simple. Hannah needs to have fifty percent or more nurses who are qualified in her package with skilled carers who have been trained and observed day in day out by the nurses, and passed some kind of competency programme. Forget about the cost, this child deserves it. We all know she won't be around forever and I don't want her to leave us due to someone's incompetence and lack of care. I mean no disrespect to the care packages but enough is enough. Look at the gap between PICU nurses and the private care packages. I can see it and now I have pointed it out, so can you."

It was all that needed to be said. I had gained the attention of everyone in the room and there was no way it could be argued that I was wrong. We waited a few weeks after that meeting and the decision was made. Hannah would go back into hospital PICU while a new package of fifty percent nurses and fifty percent domiciliary nurses were employed and trained to the standard of the NHS.

I had achieved my goal of getting the right care for Hannah which would allow Nicola, Hannah and Alice to have, at home, the best family atmosphere the circumstances would allow. Hannah would eventually be at home with the right trained team. Or so I thought. Only time would tell.

Finally in 2014, a meeting was planned with Fran Toller and Jane Wiles, who between them were to be the wheels to enable the PCT Package to work. I had known Jane for a while as she was in charge of all the wards. She was softly spoken, had a good head on her and wasn't the type to fluster in difficult situations. I had and still have a lot of respect for her. She had known me long before I knew her. She knew my name possibly through Nicola, or I may have even been in meetings long ago with her and I had not realised. What I did know is that when I had the meeting some weeks ago when I spoke on Hannah's behalf in front of all those people, she had been there and nodded as I had said my piece in relation to Hannah's care. Deep down she was the one I wanted to acknowledge my concerns as it was Jane who would be instrumental in building the ideal package.

I had never met Fran before. She was straight to the point, had a good management head on her, and seemed like the sort who took no crap off anyone. It was a Friday afternoon and both me and Nicola sat in Fran's small office while Jane explained the package and the length of time she expected it to take to start. It was going to take a while but during this time there were no issues with Hannah being on the ward as she had been on and off for the past few years.

Hannah had a band of nurses in the PICU, who you could always rely on, who were known as 'The Pinkenators', a name Hannah made up as pink was her favourite colour so she decided that would be the name of her selected team. Although Hannah could be provided with any nurse, it seemed her favourites always ended up in her corner looking after her. Helen Davidson was, in anyone's mind, no doubt Hannah's favourite nurse. They genuinely loved each other. Helen would come in to work and lean over and kiss Hannah, hug her and talk to her like a long lost little sister. It was beautiful to watch.

When Helen first came in to PICU, the time Hannah had just arrived from Newcastle, she recalled that Hannah had a tendency to not get on well with new nurses and she dreaded being the named nurse to look after her, but as time went by they became very close. If Hannah knew Helen was working, she would ask Helen to make sure she was in her corner. If Hannah wasn't well and Helen came in or one of the other Pinkenators, I felt better that she would be looked after maybe a little better. I know all the nurses gave Hannah the best care but certain PICU nurses went above and beyond. I think that's why they were singled out as Pinkenators. Rachel, Helen and Kerry were in this team along with many others.

The wait was going to be long as the new nurses came in and the carers were trained to look after Hannah at home. Immediately you could see the difference in care. This was what we had waited for and fought for all this time. Hannah's new package would have a dedicated manager with clinical care, a lady called Vicky, who had known Hannah for years. Vicky had seen all the other packages collapse and sat in so many meetings and witnessed the empty promises that were forever vocalised throughout these meetings. There was also a clinical nurse again who knew Hannah so well and had cared for her previously so she knew everything about Hannah and would become the nurse in charge. Her name was Cecelia and she was honest and trustworthy, and most importantly Hannah loved her from when she previously had taken care of her.

Things were going well. Along came Alice and Lois, two great carers who would hang in there till the end. Abbie came along later. She was a right chatterbox but had a heart of gold. Janet was another nurse who stayed till the end. She was old school, very thorough but, again, a great women. Many others came and went, but it just wasn't for them. They tried but looking back it must have been difficult to carry out so much intensive training in the environment they were in.

During the wait for the package to be complete, the PICU nurses were always there as the back-up. Without these angels I honestly don't know how Hannah would have coped. The new package was coming along okay. It had a few setbacks but it seemed to be heading in the right direction. As time went by, the package was becoming closer to allow more time at home, which was good because Hannah was also wanting to come round my house when she was home. This was a massive step in the right direction, home and even wanting to come round my house too. This was good.

Hannah did the best she could under the circumstances, and she coped so well with being pulled, prodded, turned and rolled onto her sides by new personnel daily, but deep down she knew that she would be home soon.

During the time she was at the hospital, a bus would come and collect her, supplied by Redcar and Cleveland Council and take her to Kirkleatham School in Redcar. Due to her disabilities there was no way she could attend any other school. This was the only one that had the resources available for her needs. She was welcomed by all even though she could only spend a few hours there with her carers as they had to wait with her due to her complex and specialist needs. I was invited once and spent an afternoon in the classroom with the kids. It was an unbelievable experience. The children sang karaoke and I had the pleasure of listening to Hannah sing along with the other children, a beautiful experience, and I did have a tear in my eye and was so glad I was there.

Behind the scenes so many people were doing so much for Hannah. Linda Sidgwick and her team of physios had even arranged for Hannah to have access to a trampoline at Kirkleatham School. It would involve Nicola kneeling with Hannah laid horizontal with her head being supported between Nicolas knees. The ventilator would be placed at the side of the trampoline with an extended tube, Linda and Julie would stand either side of Hannah's legs with each of them supporting each other by placing their hands on each other's shoulders, and they would then slowly start a rhythm together, slowly bouncing together. Hannah would enjoy this, but I knew I had to have a go with Hannah and take it to the extreme.

Hannah knew when I was to do this with her it would be as much fun as it was with Nicola but knew I would want to risk going further, and although she would protest at first she knew I would keep her safe. As I kneeled with Hannah's head between my knees, Linda and Julie started the rhythm slowly, then I urged them to go faster and faster. Although Hannah was blind and paralysed and couldn't feel anything but her cheeks being rubbed and my grip a little harder to keep her safe while we bounced, she loved it. The physios were sweating buckets but laughed. I loved the fact Hannah was so happy.

During this time Nicola had given birth to a little girl and called her Matilda. It was obvious this would cause more strain for Nicola as Matilda got older, but at the time the focus was Hannah, and Nicola was trying her best to juggle between the two.

I realised in this time that Hannah and me became closer and closer. It was like we were back to the old days pre-sight loss. We would sit for hours talking. The nurses would leave us alone and we would chat about everything, even my old dog Rocky who grew up with me and that he was in heaven and heaven was a beautiful place. I told her that Rocky had died a long time ago. He was old, he had lost his sight, but when he arrived in heaven, his sight returned and he could run around like he did before because in heaven nobody was ill. In reality I was trying to make Hannah feel more comfortable with the thought of heaven. It was my way of preparing her in case she ever thought of her own death but never wanted to ask anyone due to her not wanting to upset anyone. She had mentioned death years ago when she was on her way to Newcastle RVI so she was fully aware of what could happen through illness.

Those conversations we had in Hannah's last year of life were the most special moments I have ever experienced and ever will. We would talk about so much. We would laugh, and I would try to be as positive as I could at all times. Jeremy Kyle became a big favourite for Hannah. It was Alice who introduced her to the show by explaining everything about it and describing the people who would come on. It was funny.

Hannah joined Twitter and we tried to get some famous people to add her. Some did, some ignored, but that's life, I suppose. Hannah enjoyed comedy films so I came up with an idea to tweet Judd Apatow, writer, producer and actor of so many comedies: Ron Burgundy, Anchorman, Anchorman Two, Pineapple Express and many many more. He is also married to a lady called Leslie Mann who is also a comedy actress. Despite all his followers and busy schedule, he always replied to Hannah.

During the years Hannah was at the hospital, she did many things that could never be even considered for a child with so many complex issues. Credit to Nicola should be considered here as I wouldn't have thought Hannah could have been capable of so much.

On Hannah's thirteenth birthday, she was lowered in to a hydro pool, complete with long tubes attached to her ventilator. In her mind she was swimming. She was allowed on the ice skating ring in her wheelchair when the PICU nurses and family went to the skating rink for her fourteenth birthday. This was all organised by her mam and Alice. Not only this but Hannah would now be going to concerts. Rihanna, Nicki Minaj were two she attended but the best concert she went to was the Jessie J concert where she got to meet her in person on her 15th birthday, organised by Nicola. It was strange, I don't know how it came about but I received a call from Alice to say, "Dad, you never guess what? My mam and Hannah have just gone to meet Jessie J."

"So where are you?" I asked.

"Oh, it was only two people allowed so I'm just stood in the corridor."

"Right," I told her, "you knock on that door, you tell them you are Hannah's sister and her carer, and if they say you're not allowed in, put me on the phone and I'll convince them."

The security allowed it and in went Alice to meet Jessie J with Hannah and her mam.

After Jessie J met Hannah, she went on stage and spoke for a few minutes, obviously referencing Hannah but without using her name. The video was a YouTube success with many people trying to work out who she was talking about. Alice told me later that when Jessie J was talking on stage, Hannah replied, "She's talking about me!"

Hannah even got the chance to meet Prince Charles twice when he visited Redcar. The first occasion was on the sea front and he had a picture taken with her as she sat in her wheelchair with Nicola and carers. The second time she was in the crowd again, sitting in her wheelchair but this time as Prince Charles was about to get in his car, he spotted her in the crowd with her pink blanket covering her and decided to walk up and talk to her.

It was around then that I decided to plan something myself. I ordered tickets for The Lion, the Witch and the Wardrobe at the Little Theatre, Middlesbrough. It wasn't far from the hospital but this was my test. I could carry out the basics, Nicola would drop us off in her vehicle and we would not be far away in the event she was needed. All bases were covered. It was planned for a Saturday matinee session, and would be the first time I had been alone with Hannah, with the exception of a nurse in the background, outside of her house and the PICU since the time in late November 2005 when we stood and watched the sun come up together. I was also reassured by the package manager that everything was in place and a named nurse deemed competent by the new package competency system was all set to come with me. I couldn't wait and neither could Hannah.

I called at the hospital on the Saturday morning to find the named nurse who had been training for over three solid months was unwell. Luckily, Rachel the PICU nurse was the nurse in charge that day and moved heaven and earth to get us to the theatre. She organised for Kate Howe, a lovely, great PICU nurse who had looked after Hannah on and off for a couple of years, to come with us.

It was a brilliant show, and during the interval I went to the dressing room area and asked the actors to come and speak to Hannah. I briefly explained her condition and the fact she knew the show off by heart, word for word due to it being her favourite film of all time. They were great with Hannah. I took pictures and Hannah loved every minute they were there and talked about it nonstop to every nurse or carer that came on duty for weeks.

Around this time, Cecelia discovered she was pregnant and had to leave the package for some time. I had decided to extend my home to allow Hannah to visit and have overnight stays, and Nicola agreed this would be a good idea as she had Matilda and help from my end would be beneficial. The plans were put together and the team involved visited my home to assess the needs for hoisting equipment and other medical essentials. As Hannah already had a suitable home with the essential equipment, there would be no funds available to allow such an extension and would have to be paid for directly by me. I was aware at the start this would be a costly exercise but I didn't care. If I could share access on the month I was home from my cycle offshore, I didn't care. Hannah had been round a few times already and enjoyed it. The garden was big and we would sit outside listening to the birds. I would explain what they looked like as Pepsi the dog we had bought a few years previously was hanging around barking at everything that moved. Hannah loved it.

Previous to coming to my house, on occasions she would come with me to the Kingfisher Pub in Dormanstown when she was home with the new package, and had done with the previous packages. It was close to her house, the ramps would be put in place and the lads would all open the doors to allow her to sit with them.

Hannah met a good friend in the pub, a girl who was around her age. The girl was playing pool. I started them talking to each other and then she came over and started talking to Hannah. Her name was Rosie Burniston, a girl with a heart of gold who would eventually come round to sit and talk to Hannah for hours. Not only this but I would sometimes pick her up and take her to the hospital to visit Hannah. They became very close and it was nice to witness a girl around the same age keeping Hannah up to speed with the latest on what was going on around the area. She was a good, genuine friend of Hannah's who just never stopped talking, which Hannah enjoyed.

Hannah was at home for her 16th birthday and was due to come to mine for a small tea party. It was always difficult to find a gift for Hannah. No matter how hard you tried, it was so difficult to find something for a girl with no sight, and no feeling from the neck down, but on this occasion I thought of something that she would love. I have a friend who has pigeons and I asked him to bring two baskets of pigeons down to Hannah's house. I positioned Hannah close to the baskets laid on the floor, and I told her what I had planned. I was to release the pigeons, they would fly out, around ten to fifteen at a time and fly right past her face. She would feel the wind from their wings and hear the flap as they rushed to get in the air.

The first basket was released and they flew out by Hannah. It was fun to watch and Hannah enjoyed it, but to be safe I had pulled the basket back slightly as I didn't want them all hitting her in and around the face. I decided I would place the second basket closer and did so. The second basket of pigeons hit the spot. It took Hannah's breath away. It only took less than ten seconds for all the pigeons to be released but it was a perfect birthday present.

Another friend of Hannah's and Nicola's was a lady called Janice had been coming to the hospital every week for years and when Hannah was at home she would call to the house, and would stand and read to Hannah for hours on end. Hannah loved her. She had a lovely Irish accent, and I loved listening to her read to Hannah if I happened to be there.

So we'd had some great moments, but at times it felt like it was one step forward and one back. The planning application had been put in, and I anticipated the plans coming back late November, late December with a plan to start the building of the extension around January 2015. As we sat down in yet another meeting with Jane, the package manager, and Nicola (with Matilda), Jane explained there was a possibility Hannah would be more suited in an environment that was not the PICU and suggested a new development close by which had all the amenities to allow Hannah and her care team to provide the same care she was receiving in the PICU.

To be honest I was expecting something of this nature at some point. Hannah should have been at home a long time ago and should not have had to spend her life in PICU. It had become more difficult since Matilda came along for Nicola. The nurses and carers from the care package along with PICU nurses had a good routine on the morning which stretched till around 11am. This worked for Hannah also, and as a result Nicola could come up to the hospital later. It also worked in my favour because I was spending more time with Hannah when I was at the hospital.

By now the message was clear, Hannah would not be going home full time, a home fit for her needs was the first choice in Middlesbrough, with visits to my house when the extension was completed, and home to her house in Dormanstown.

The planning permission for the extension was accepted and arrived by email to me to confirm this at 5.30pm on November 25th 2014 as I sat in the front room crying and taking in what had just happened... Hannah had died three hours previous.

CHAPTER 12

Goodbye Hannah…
25th November 2014

As I write part of this final chapter I'm sitting in a hotel room in Stavanger, Norway, on November 25th 2015. Here for work. I've had an awful day but I've hidden it well. I've had messages from people showing support which I appreciate but may not have replied. I've spoken to nobody on the fact it's exactly a year to the day that Hannah left us. I've cried so much over the last year and asked questions as to why she left. I've been angry with mixed emotions that seem to get worse by the day. By completing this chapter of the book on this sad day, I seem to have found a way of closing out my emotional chapter of grief and now look forward to allowing everyone to understand just how I've felt over the last seventeen years, but, most importantly, hope that some fathers out there have gathered strength from reading this book to enable them to grasp the enormity of just what we need to do when coping with watching our children suffer. If nothing else, know you're not alone.

Towards the end, Hannah was unwell and not responding well to certain treatments. Her ventilator needed to be increased to enable her to get the breaths needed to keep things running smoothly. It was no major concern at first as everyone considered this a chest infection which, with plenty of physio from carers and nurses, would eventually fix the issue. This condition started to set alarm bells ringing when the usual time frame of events meant that when she should have been in a position to have the ventilator reduced, unfortunately this wasn't the case so we were asking the usual questions and not getting concrete information.

Around this time, Hannah's consultant, Jonathan Grimmley, asked to speak with both me and Nicola. It was during this discussion I picked out the parts of the conversation that mattered and they were the words that Hannah may not be getting better as her organs finally giving up could be a sign that was Hannah's way of saying, "It's time now." Hannah was quiet but still talkative. The pressures on her ventilator didn't seem to bother her but once again I would sit and talk to her at her bedside, not mentioning anything the consultant had told me as I had never done over the years. Some people may think this is wrong and I should have told her the truth, but why have a child worry that the last few weeks could be the last time they spend time with their father or mother or sister?

The amount of times I had been told Hannah was possibly leaving us was at least seven…

Hannah seemed to pick herself up again a couple of days later and was allowed out of the ward and down to the coffee shop to sit with her mam and carers, myself and Alice. We sat with her and had a chat. Hannah was not herself and I could see this. Little did we all know then it would be the last time Hannah left the ward.

I was due to fly to Milan for five days on a work assignment. I felt comfortable in knowing Hannah would still be cared for as she had been all the time in the past. She had her mam who would always give 110% for Hannah when she was unwell and would always keep me informed if things were not going in the right direction. Over the coming days Hannah had to have her pressures increased again. I spoke at length with the consultant and Nicola via Skype and was kept completely up to date. Even Hannah had a chat with me as she usually would via Skype so I wasn't overly concerned in the pressure increase.

On Saturday November 6th 2014, I arrived back in the UK and as usual went straight to the hospital.

I was immediately alarmed at Hannah's condition. She looked unsettled and in pain. I asked to speak with the doctors immediately to ask why Hannah was not sedated, surely the situation warranted this? It was then that I was informed that this should happen and the parameters of a child on the settings she was on with her ventilator's pressure should warrant sedation. The topic had been raised with Nicola the day before and I believe she felt that either the hospital's physios and care team could prevent this or she subconsciously felt that when this happened, Hannah may not recover. It's a topic we never discussed and I felt this needed to happen to enable Hannah to fix herself while sedated which would in turn prevent her stress levels being exceeded whilst not sedated.

I made the decision as Hannah's father to have her sedated and informed Nicola that whether she liked it or not, it was my decision and gave her the reasons why I came to this decision. After our conversation, Nicola accepted it had to be done and trusted my decision.

Throughout the day Hannah was slowly sedated. It would take time due to her weight and size to get the balance of her sedation correct. Nicola was at the hospital with her daughter Matilda, and Alice was there also quietly entertaining Hannah. I sat with Hannah when the bed space was not overcrowded, feeling relieved she would soon be sedated and be in a position to fix herself as she had done so many times in the past. Nicola, Alice and Matilda went around 7pm. I decided to stay. Hannah was quiet as the sedatives took time to work. We spoke very little. I would chat with the nurse and Hannah would listen. Her mam had gone. She loved her mam uncontrollably. I knew I was second best, as in the past I was always more strict with her.

On that night, 6th November, Hannah's allocated nurse was Rachel. I was relieved as I knew Hannah would have 100% of Rachel's attention and if there was a problem I would know about it and so would Nicola. I sat with Hannah until 8pm. I knew she didn't want to say much but I tried to no avail. I remember to this day the words I said to her. It was the last time I would ever speak to Hannah alone.

I said, "Goodnight, Hannah. You go to sleep now. I'm going to get going. I love you. Are you okay?"

"Yes," Hannah said. "Goodnight, dad. I love you too."

"I'll call you when I'm driving home," I said. "I'll come and see you tomorrow." I then kissed her on her cheek.

I had made the decision for her to be sedated and thought that by doing this it would help her stop becoming stressed and allow her to fix herself, as she had in the past.

I walked out of the hospital to the sound of fireworks going off. It was the closest Saturday to Bonfire Night so it seemed everyone had decided to use tonight as fireworks night. Marton Road was covered in smoke from the fireworks that had burnt out. As usual I rang the hospital and was told that Hannah had fallen asleep.

I called back up the next day and again spent most of the day along with Nicola, Matilda and Alice. As Hannah was now sedated, it was a waiting game. The following week started off with everything going okay then it went back over. As we waited towards the weekend, we were heading in the right direction, or so I thought. Hannah had woken briefly just before an operation to drain fluids from her and she told her mam she loved her. Her mam explained that both me and Alice were there. As I walked over and said, "Hello, Hannah," she told me to go away. For those who knew Hannah, she would often say this to me when she was ill or in a mood. I believe she wanted to blame someone for the way she was and most of the time it was me. Although we were so close as father and daughter, I was her punch bag so to speak. And as I've said already, I know that Hannah was frustrated that we couldn't do the things together that we used to when she was younger. I can only imagine how hard that must have been for her.

The operation went well and the fluids began to drain, which meant Hannah was heading in the right direction.

Even though she was heavily sedated, I looked over to her bed one afternoon during that week and Alice was reading a book to her. I asked everyone quietly to keep away from the bed as I saw this was Hannah and Alice time. Alice spent at least two hours that day sitting alone, reading the book out loud to Hannah. It was one of the nicest and most touching moments I ever witnessed.

I packed my bag Saturday night and set off for Norway offshore on the Sunday, travelling all day to a place called Hammerfest then by chopper onto the rig on the Monday. I arrived on the rig to turn on my iPad to have messages from Nicola saying Hannah was now going the opposite direction and not good.

Over the coming days she was up and down, so too was my head. As Hannah had always done this in the past, I wasn't too worried but kept in touch to have a finger on the pulse. On the Wednesday of that week a new platform manager came on to the rig. He knew about Hannah as I had briefly discussed her with him the last time I was on the rig, and it so happened he had been in similar situations with his son who needed care also. I immediately brought him up to speed with the situation and said if things deteriorated I would need to leave. In other words, I would need a chopper to get me off. I knew he would sort it.

The weekend of November 22nd/23rd 2014 came and Hannah was still going in the right direction. Then on the morning of November 24th, I received a text message from Nicola saying, "You need to come home." I always appreciated Nicola keeping me up to speed but in the past I'd travelled many miles when I was told the worst, only to get there and find that Hannah was okay. Looking back now, I can see Nicola needed support. On this occasion I rang the hospital to talk to Dr Grimmley. He wasn't there but by chance Rachel answered. I asked her what was going on and if I should come home, and she said it wasn't looking good. I came off the phone and told my manager the situation. I didn't know what to do, I'd been in this situation before, and honestly didn't know what to do. I asked him what he'd do.

He said, "I would go home, that's why I'm sending you off the rig. Trust me, you need to go. We will sort the chopper. Get your stuff sorted. You have an hour and you're gone."

It was exactly what I needed.

I needed a push, so that was it. I was leaving. The only problem was I needed to catch four flights from the top of Norway to Durham Tees Valley.

Hammerfest to Tromso, then Tromso to Trondheim, an

overnight in Trondheim, then Trondheim to Amsterdam, then Amsterdam to Durham Tees Valley where my usual taxi driver Terry would be there to get me to the hospital at breakneck speed. It was the only way back to the UK.

With a chopper coming at 1pm that meant I wouldn't get home until 9am the next morning.

It wasn't until I spoke to the Jonathan Grimmley via FaceTime on the night in Trondheim did I realise just how serious it was. I was told the ventilator would be switched off tomorrow regardless as it was so serious and keeping Hannah alive was not the thing to do. Her organs had failed and she would never recover. I was informed that there was a chance she could even leave us of her own accord that night.

I had to get back to say goodbye.

If I hadn't been able to I honestly don't think I would have been able to write this book, the guilt would have been too much.

I knew this day would eventually come. It had been in the back of my mind for a long time. As the years had gone by, I would say to Hannah, "Hannah, if you're ever fast asleep but want to wake up but can't because you are feeling drowsy, I will rub my face on you and you will know it's me because of my whiskers." She would laugh, but really I was saying if you're ever sedated and it's coming to the end, you will know it's me.

I arrived at the hospital and was met at the doors by Alice. It was evident she had been up most of the night.

We hugged and walked up to the ward and into PICU, not saying a great deal to each other but I could see she was relieved I had made it. Over the years when a child was going to die, I had witnessed them going into a side room where it would be much more peaceful and respectful for the families. The main PICU ward is split into two large rooms, the main room where Hannah had stayed on her previous visit in 2007 when she came from Newcastle General and spent a year, and then the other room where it adjoins the main room but is slightly out of the way but close enough in the event there is an emergency.

Hannah had the pleasure of having her own bed space in the adjoining room and was allowed posters up of her favourite singer, Nicki Minaj. On this day a sheet had been placed up to separate the rooms. The nurses who had cared for Hannah and genuinely loved her had come in on their days off to work to be with us all to make the day as easy as possible.

I walked in and immediately thanked everyone for being there and then asked if everyone could leave the room while I spent time alone with Hannah.

They all did including Alice and Nicola. I began by rubbing my whiskers on Hannah and at the same time observed the monitors to see if there was a reaction... nothing.

I talked to her and remember every single word. It lasted five minutes or so but I knew it was the last time I would ever be alone with her and I savoured every moment. This time she didn't reply, but I knew in my heart she heard me.

Throughout the morning the nurses had put together memory boxes for all three of us. Within the boxes were lockets of Hannah's hair and tiny finger print mugs. Throughout this time I observed the pure love these nurses had for Hannah. There was Karen who had tap danced on Christmas Day all those years ago. Helen, Hannah's best friend over the last few years. Rachel who went above and beyond when it came to Hannah's care and equally loved Hannah as much as Hannah loved Rachel. Maria who had always been such brilliant support for Nicola and Alice in identifying and pointing out points in Hannah's care that were required. She spoke with such a soft natured voice but always considered Hannah first and if Nicola or myself didn't like it then tough, we knew she was putting Hannah first. And lastly, we had Tracy, one of the original nurses right from day one and whenever she came into work back in 1998 and 1999, we always hoped she had Hannah due to her caring side. I would not have wanted any other people there that day than those five nurses. I will always have a special part in my heart for them and have the utmost respect for them and all the other staff linked with PICU.

Dr Grimmley came in at one point in the early afternoon and pulled me and Nicola to the side and said, "I'm sorry but we need to consider letting Hannah leave us within the next hour," or words to that effect.

The end was close.

It hit me like a punch.

Alice came to me and asked if she could lay on the bed

with Hannah when the ventilator was turned off. I agreed as I knew Nicola would want to, so I spoke with Nicola and she agreed, even though I knew she wanted to be the one to lay next to her. We didn't want Alice would be on the outside, struggling to get in. And as hard as it was for all of us, Alice was her sister and they were close.

The time was 2.10pm and we were told we needed to go to the bedside. Dr Grimmley asked us if we were ready. Alice lay on the bed, Nicola was next to Alice and had her hand stretched over Alice and had it resting on Hannah's heart. I stood at the other side of the bed. I was just wanting to observe and was standing next to Rachel and Helen. Tracy was at the end of the bed and Maria was standing alongside Nicola. In front of me was Dr Grimmley. He turned round and gently guided me closer and told me to hold Hannah's hand. I shouldn't have needed to be prompted but I was probably in a state of shock and wasn't ready to watch my daughter's life slip away. It should have been the other way round. No parent should ever be in this position. Unfortunately I was.

Karen and Dr Grimmley worked in unison, lowering the ventilator, and within a minute or so it was over.

Nicola and Alice were heartbroken and were crying so much. I turned to the nurses to find every one of them had broken down. Despite knowing Hannah for the longest, Karen kept herself together while she and the doctor carried out the correct procedure to enable everything to be recorded correctly.

I needed air. I had to leave the hospital. I went outside

and rang Janine. She was the one who had listened to me over the years and was probably the only person I had cried in front of when it came to Hannah. I told her that Hannah had left us and then cried, sitting on a bench alone and away from everyone. People walked by, oblivious to me, going about their daily routines. Janine stayed on the phone, knowing I couldn't talk. She waited patiently until I was ready to talk again, and after five minutes or so I told her I needed to go and would call her for a lift home when I was ready.

I called my mam next and asked her to call the family rather than me having to call anyone. I started to cry again, along with my mam, who couldn't believe what she was hearing. Unfortunately it was true. Hannah had finally decided it was time for us all to let her go peacefully and in her sleep.

I had called my best mate Jonny earlier in the day when I had to go outside for some air and told him what was going to be happening later that day. He immediately made the decision to not go offshore the next day but to come round to my house to support me. I told him I would be okay but he insisted and I'm glad he did in the end. It's strange how grief works, and as we had known each other for over thirty eight years, he must have known I would need support from all directions.

As I walked up the PICU corridor, the lady who would bring us parents cups of tea and coffee saw me. She had heard what had happened and immediately looked at me and burst into tears. The whole ward outside PICU was in shock. When I went back in to PICU, I looked for Alice and hugged her so tight. She was still upset. I told her I loved her so much and that Hannah was now in a better place, hoping she would understand. All the nurses were still upset and we all hugged. Nicola was sitting on the floor with Caroline, the manager of PICU, both were upset and hugging. Everyone was in shock but we knew it was the right thing to have done.

I looked at Hannah and her pallor was changing colour which meant that she would soon be going to the morgue. I wanted my memory of her to be in PICU, not being wheeled to the morgue through the hospital so I decided to leave and asked Alice to come with me. Alice wanted to stay with her mam and Matilda. Matilda had been taken for a walk by Jaime the PICU helper. The last thing Nicola needed was to have to take care of Matilda during the time the ventilator was to be turned off and this was a nice gesture by the ward to do this.

I still had my offshore bags with me and said goodbye to everyone and thanked them for their support and care. Rachel walked with me to the main entrance to help with my bags whilst everyone continued with their thoughts in the ward. We hugged and I thanked her from the bottom of my heart for the support and care she had shown for Hannah. She had always gone above and beyond, and I'll never forget her dedication. I then turned and walked outside.

As I turned the corner, the sky was a pinky colour. At the time I didn't think anything about it. Later that night Helen sent both me and Nicola a picture of the sky she had taken while she was out getting some air, with the caption, "This is Hannah saying I've arrived." She couldn't have been more true. The sky was pink, Hannah's favourite colour.

I was picked up by Janine and her friend Rachel. I was quiet in the car and didn't say a great deal. My phone rang. It was Nicola. We had to make a decision now whether we were to bury or cremate Hannah. I was shocked at the urgency. I left the decision to her, hoping she would go for the latter in which she did. We were to meet with the funeral directors at Nicola's house the next day to organise this.

The funeral was organised and the vicar, Bruce, even came out of retirement to cremate Hannah due to a request by me and Nicola as he had met Hannah on so many occasions. I tasked myself with directing the whole church service and spent half a day at the church on the Saturday 7th December with Bruce, Martin the sound technician who arranged songs and Sid, an old fella who was the key holder of the church and also carried out admin. Together the scene was set for a memorable day on Monday 8th December 2014, white horses with pink manes, white carriage, and a pink coffin.

The week leading up to the funeral, Hannah was in the chapel of rest at Guisborough. I arrived to go in and see her and started talking to the receptionist. She suddenly broke down and continued to apologise profusely. I asked what was up and she replied, "I've heard so much about your daughter over the years and followed her stories in the Evening Gazette of how she has continuously fought back and I'm just so sorry she has gone." Now this was a woman who worked in the trade and was crying her eyes out. Me being me, I switched modes and comforted her then went in to see Hannah.

I cried alone and could see Nicola had been making everything perfect along with the staff. It just looked like Hannah was asleep. Nicola had put a note inside the coffin to Hannah. The words were lovely.

Over the next few days, myself and Janine would call in to see Hannah and talk to her. Nicola, Matilda and Alice would call up also and spend a lot of time there, saying their last goodbyes. It was evident Nicola was struggling more than anyone, but this was to be expected as she had spent so much time with Hannah.

The day of the funeral arrived. We met at Nicola's house as we would have two cars behind the horse and carriage, myself, Janine, Sean, Alice, Nicola and Matilda in the first car followed by Nicola's family in the second car. Everyone else including my family would meet at the church, and everybody had to wear something with pink in it, that was our only request.

The carriage arrived. It was beautiful, an absolute tribute to what Hannah would have wanted. We set off a journey of around one mile. Everyone stopped. Council workers who were working took off their hats as a mark of respect. I watched a DHL delivery man in the distance, oblivious to our horse and carriage, park his van abruptly on the pavement, get out and run up a drive to deliver a parcel. By the time he came back down the drive, we were alongside him. It was obvious he was in a rush but he stopped, bowed his head in respect, and as his head came up, he made eye contact with me in the car and we both nodded at each other. I was saying thank you, he was acknowledging me. It's amazing the things you remember.

I turned to Nicola in the car and asked her if she would be getting up and speaking. She said she had not prepared anything. I knew she wouldn't because she'd been spending so much time at the chapel of rest, so I pulled out a piece of paper. It was the note she had left in Hannah's coffin. I'd taken a photo of it and printed it off. Her words needed to be heard. I knew Alice had prepared something as she was running it by me leading up to the funeral, and her words were to be just as beautiful and came from the heart.

We arrived at the church. I knew there would be a lot of people there but I was shocked to see so many people outside. Everyone had something which was pink either attached to their clothing or wearing something pink. As the coffin was pulled from the carriage, I decided I wanted to help carry Hannah into the church. I knew I wouldn't be in a fit state to do this after the service so decided I would do it going into the church. My concentration was fixed on the coffin going into the church and I was unaware of the amount of people in the church until we positioned the coffin down and I turned round. The church was packed full. A sea of pink could be seen all around.

The vicar, Bruce, spoke first using words I had written, then Nicola spoke, then myself and lastly Alice. Bruce completed the service, then the song from the movie Frozen was played as we left the church to begin our journey to the crematorium.

I knew for years in my heart I would be standing and talking about Hannah at her funeral. So many people have asked me since how could I compose myself as well as I did. The reason for this is because I had years of preparation.

Below is the extract I prepared and read out. There was sadness and humour. I hope you understand this father's last message.

"Today is a celebration of Hannah's life. Those who had the privilege of knowing Hannah have been blessed. She would touch the heart of everyone she met. Before I talk about Hannah, I want to thank some individuals. If I have forgotten anyone, I apologise now. Firstly, let me thank everyone here for coming to pay respect to a much loved girl. The cards you have sent to me, the messages on Facebook. And thank you to my friends who I've shared a drink with over the years, whether it be up Lingdale, Boosbeck, Dormanstown or Redcar. You know I never ever discussed Hannah and none of you ever asked me about her. Thank you for that, but now is the time that I will talk.

Nineteen years ago, my best friend was born, Alice Dowson. Three years later my other best friend was born, Hannah Dowson.

The love I have for those two individuals is and always will be the strongest I will ever imagine.

Throughout the years Hannah has been ill, Alice would go to sleep laid by her sister and wake up on occasions in another house, whether it be her nana's or my house. Then she would ask the question 'where is Hannah?' Was she ill overnight? Where's my mam? Where's dad? To be told by either her nana, her Aunty Kendra or Janine, my wife, that Hannah had to go to hospital.

So not only was Hannah suffering physically, there was a little girl who was suffering mentally. Alice has grown up into a beautiful and sensible young woman. Throughout her life she has attended acting schools and acting college. I believe that one day she will tell the world about her sister, the brave, witty, courageous, and beautiful sister she had the pleasure of spending sixteen years with. Alice, thank you for being you. You are my life.

I'd like to thank Nicola, an excellent mother who spent her life caring for Hannah. Some mothers would have folded and given in. She never did. She fought and fought for the best care for her daughter, Hannah. Some understood her plight, others thought she was just a pain. Let me ask you this: if your daughter or son suddenly became ill which meant that your child would need your full attention and care for the next 3285 days (nine years) and your house became a house in which hundreds of individuals would be in and out with a large percentage of staff not understanding Hannah's needs due to sometimes incompetent managers from the private sector care packages, how would you be? She's a mother who has done an excellent job caring for my daughter and I will always have the utmost respect for you, Nicola. Thank you.

I'd like to thank my wife, Janine. She doesn't say a great deal but is an excellent listener. I would moan and whine, and cry to her about Hannah, and she was always there. I would be home on leave and spend so much time at the hospital that we hardly saw each other, but she knew there was no way I would ever not see Hannah at the hospital or visit her at her home. When I decided to get an extension at our new house, she was 100% supportive as she knew I needed to have Hannah sleeping at mine with her pool of carers. She knew as well as I did that Hannah wouldn't be here forever so my time was precious with her. Thank you, Janine. I love you.

The NHS staff. What can I say? I hope there is no one needing their appendices out today because two thirds of the NHS staff are in here. There is a collection when we leave so dig deep: this is for the PICU staff.

I could go on forever thanking everyone who looked after my daughter. The PICU staff in particular were the heart of my daughter's care. Whenever a care package collapsed, in jumped the PICU staff, wonderful women and Mike Carr. The Pinkenators, you know who you are. Helen, Hannah's other sister, you were brilliant. The relationship you had with Hannah was unreal. Rachel, Karen Coates, Maria, Maxine, Kerry Foxtrot, your sense of humour, the laughs we had, Carol Ann, forever reminding me I used to drive buses. I could go on all day.

The new care package, Lois, Alice, Janet, and Sophie, you hung in there. You knew how desperate we were to get Hannah home so thank you. And Abbey, a young girl who only arrived with the package some months ago, the fact you knew Hannah hadn't looked good for a while, you went out of your way to plait and sort her hair and makeup while she had been sedated for so long. I walked in and said, "Rachel must be on duty because she would always make Hannah look like this," but was told no it was Abbey. That in itself is something I will never forget as it's a memory I have now that will stay with me forever. You made her look even more beautiful.

Jane Whiles for placing no pressure on Hannah to stay in PICU and being instrumental in the new package. Cecelia, for your determination on striving to get the package working yet working alone. Myself and Nicola fought for years for the NHS package and in the end we got it, so thank you Jane, Fran Toller and Khalid for being part of this new package.

Fiona Hampton, and Johnathan Grimmley, Hannah's consultant, thank you for listening to me. For the first time I felt that I had been listened to. I'll always have the utmost respect for you and the way you conducted yourself as Hannah's consultant, and keeping her there for me so I could get back to spend those remaining hours with Hannah.

But the reason we're here... I want to talk about Hannah and celebrate her life, and concentrate on the fun times. For those in here who were lucky enough to have met Hannah before her sight loss, there were so many fun times and I'm sure you will have heard some of the stories but I'm going to talk about these now:

- 'Who do you love the most?' 'Something Hannah would say.
- The school play... demanding I come and sit at the front, embarrassing me.
- Cigarettes from Bells Stores. When I was with Hannah buying cigarettes and the woman wouldn't serve me because Hannah had been in the day before and told them not to serve me, describing me as tall, spikey hair and a big nose.

- *Hutton le Hole picnic where Hannah tried to drown Alice in the stream because Alice wouldn't share the towel.*
- *Holiday in Florida, when Hannah locked me and Alice out and we had to break in through a small window.*
- *The bungee catapult where Hannah was catapulted into the air with me. At the time it was the largest in the world, she saw no danger.*
- *Swimming with dolphins in Florida.*
- *The parking ticket and handcuffs incident. I had the kids at the amusement's one night. We noticed a flash and looked outside, and the traffic police had issued me with a parking ticket as the disabled badge wasn't showing. As I contested this, Hannah tapped the traffic man on the leg and said, "Do you have handcuffs?" to which he replied, "No, why?" Hannah said, "I wanted to see my dad being put in handcuffs like on the TV."*
- *McDonald's and lying about her being there that morning. I took Hannah out for a walk one Sunday afternoon in her wheelchair. I asked if she was hungry which she said she was. I then said we can go to McDonald's if you want as long as you haven't been this morning with your mam. She said she hadn't. We went inside, sat down, and as we were eating the McDonald's, the cleaner came up to Hannah and said, "Hello you, that's twice you have been in here today." Hannah just bowed her head, and I chuckled under my breath. Typical Hannah.*
- *Swinging Patch round. Patch was around twelve weeks old. Janine was upstairs and heard a constant banging. She went downstairs to find Hannah swinging Patch around by his collar and letting him go. He would then fly across the floor and hit the table and chairs. Janine said, "Ohh Hannah, I don't think you should be*

doing that," to which Hannah replied, "No it's okay, he likes it. Look, he keeps coming back for more." The truth was he did like it and did keep coming back for more.

• *Standing in a cow pat. The time a herd of cows chased me, Alice, Sean and Hannah across a field. Seconds before, Hannah decided to stand on a dry cow pat so it was now all over her shoes. Because she couldn't run, I had to put her on my shoulders and run.*

• *Jonny Parker having small metal toy cars thrown at him by Hannah, narrowly missing his head.*

• *Watching the sun come up and the pheasants talking to you. My best memory was two weeks before you lost your sight. We got up at 06:30, got ready and took Patch rabbiting. When we walked up a hill and got to the top, the sun was just coming up. We stopped to watch this and you turned to me and said, "Wow dad, that is beautiful," and in return I replied, "Not many kids your age will ever witness that. They will see it go down but they aren't up at this time of morning to witness it coming up. Remember this moment, Hannah, as it will stay with you for a long time."*

• *Jeremy Kyle. The time I bought you an uncut Jeremy Kyle DVD and we watched it on the ward and the two women and one bloke were arguing and the one women said, "So what about when you were shagging me in the garage?" and you said, "Who got stabbed in the garage?" Without thinking, I said, "No, shagging." "What's shagging?" I was like a rabbit in the headlights. I had to act quickly and said, "It's when a man and woman rub bellies together." You laughed so much. You knew what I was talking about.*

Hannah, you have been my life. You are the last thing I think of on a night and the first thing I think of on a morning. I will never

ever forget the joy you brought to me. I'm broken but I can be fixed in time.

When you started to break, I knocked on the doors of consultants with an envelope of your MRI scan pictures and list of illnesses. I've had heated arguments with consultants, asking them why they can't give me answers to fix you. I've had emails from consultants from America telling me that the NHS have done and are doing the best anyone can do. I've been asked to leave hospitals in the Middle East after confronting consultants on top wages and then producing a summary of your notes and then demanding they now earn their wages and give me answers.

I will miss our deep conversations of just me and you talking and laughing about everything. The way we would take the piss out of people, the stories you always used to ask me to make up about the animals taking away a little girl to help injured animals in their pack, and then bring her back to her dad who had spent weeks looking for her, and as the animals left, they would turn around and say, "What's your name?" and you would finish the story by saying "My name is Hannah Mae Dowson."

You never knew just how famous you are Hannah. On a flight back from Dubai, I was sitting next to a doctor. We got chatting, she asked me my name and immediately asked if I was related to you. She worked in Newcastle and had heard so much about you.

We've been told to prepare for you leaving us so many times but you have continuously baffled the world of medical knowledge. No parent should ever have to let their child go but I have. You knew deep down but we never discussed it. We went around it by talking about Heaven and how Rocky (my old dog) could see now in heaven and that anyone who was ill would be better when they reached heaven.

Hannah, thank you for being you. Thank you for being my daughter. You are at rest now, no more medication, no more operations, no more alarms going off on your ventilator. You can now play up there, being the mischievous kid you are. No doubt you will be having fun up there.

After you left us on the 25th, I left the hospital in a daze and looked up at the sky. It was a red sky at night but it was mainly a stunning pink colour. It was such a mystery that the Gazette ran pictures of it the next day commenting on it. It wasn't a mystery, let me tell you all now. That was Hannah saying, 'I've arrived.'

I love you so much, Hannah, and always will. I'm lost without you and don't know how I'm going to get by but I will. I just want to say it's been an honour and privilege to have been part of your life."

After I'd finished, Alice spoke of her love for her sister and the enjoyment she had experienced with her sister over the years. We left the church to a song which Hannah loved from the film Frozen, Let It Go.

Before we left, every PICU nurse walked up to the coffin and placed a single rose on the coffin. It brought a tear to my eye as it was such a beautiful gesture. They all walked past me in doing this and I remember one of the nurses, Kate, hugging me and giving me a kiss on the cheek. It was a beautiful gesture from someone who had given everything she could to care for Hannah when she was in her care over the years, as had many of the other nurses there at the church.

After leaving the church we made our way to Kirkleatham Crematorium. The journey would pass many people who stopped and removed caps or simply bowed their head in respect. The service was not long due to the time we had spent in the church, which I believe was my fault because of the time I spent talking about my love for Hannah and the good times we had.

As I sat at the front of the crematorium with Janine by my side, I looked out of the window as the coffin disappeared behind a curtain. It's something I didn't want to see. Instead I listened to the words of Bruce the vicar and looked over the field towards Dunsdale, the area where both me and Hannah had stood on that November morning nine years before as we watched the sun come up… the best memory of Hannah and dad time ever.

EPILOGUE

Know You're Not Alone…
February 2020

My intention in writing this book was to express my feelings and to enable other fathers in my position to relate and hopefully take some comfort in knowing they are not alone. This book has taken six years to write, and it would never have been completed if I hadn't bumped into a friend by chance and told her I had written two chapters of the story about me and Hannah. She asked me to send the two chapters, and after reading these she insisted I finish the book. Thank you, Kerry. Your advice has helped me through the grieving process.

So what has happened since November 2014? I struggled for years and hid it well. I cried alone and wished I had done more to help. I watched Nicola and Alice, who I think seemed to cope, but they were equally as heartbroken as me. I watched Janine struggle as I had completely shut her out and didn't want to know her at times. She hung in there as she knew the pain I was in. She would tell me years later that she could her me crying in another room. I had counselling to help me grieve and understand the process of grief and it helped, although at the time I didn't think so.

Then on June 4th 2016 something magical happened. Alice gave birth to a little girl she named Felicity. She came for a reason, I believe, and from day one she has been a big part in both mine and Janine's life. Alice was a wonderful sister and she is a fantastic mam. She settled down with a nice lad called James, and although he is not Felicity's biological father, he does a great job as her dad. In August 2020, Alice and James are to give birth to their own child.

And as for Hannah… she continues to live in our hearts, and will do so forever.